COURTNEY

FEMININE ARCHETYPES

REMEMBER, RECLAIM, AND EMBODY YOUR TRUTH

First paperback edition May 2021

Edited by Lyric Dodson
Book cover design by Margo Craige
Book interior design by Ines Monnet

Paperback ISBN: 978-1-7349209-4-9
E-book ISBN: 978-1-7349209-5-6

Aligned Life Publishing
PO Box 72623
Phoenix, AZ 85050

www.courtneytiffany.com

For Daphne

Discovering your archetype is like being introduced to yourself at the soul level.

— Carolyn Myss

CONTENTS

Introduction 1

The Maiden 9

The Wild Woman 19

The Warrior 35

The Huntress 47

The Lover 59

The Witch 83

The Mother 99

The Queen 111

The Priestess 121

The Hearth Keeper 133

The Dark Goddess 145

The Mystic 157

The Crone 167

Conclusion 177

Acknowledgements 181

About the Author 183

Resources to Deepen Your Journey 184

INTRODUCTION

Carl Jung first explored archetypes back in the 1940s, recognizing that there were common universal themes within the collective unconscious. Jungian psychology explored the themes we all are familiar with in society, such as the maiden, the hero, the caregiver, and the magician. I first began exploring the idea of these archetypes at the beginning of my spiritual journey in 2016 to better understand myself. Then, I came across Jean Shinoda Bolen's book *Goddesses in Everywoman*, where she examined the archetypes of the Greek goddesses from her viewpoint as a Jungian psychoanalyst. After that, I dove deep into mythology, goddesses, and the energy of the Divine Feminine. Common archetypes within the goddesses started appearing to me, far from those of Carl Jung, and I chose to explore them within myself. These are the feminine archetypes we will be exploring in this book. It was these very archetypes that allowed me to put the pieces of myself back together and reclaim my sovereignty, esoteric gifts, and feminine power.

Now, I am no psychoanalyst, and these are not Jung's archetypes. I am simply a woman on a lifelong mission to learn, grow, and find my personal truth, constantly realigning and course-correcting who I am at my core. What I uncovered was that there are powerful feminine archetypes available to each and every one of us, and we can learn to energetically tap into them to reconnect with parts of ourselves that might have otherwise been dormant or hidden, parts we've forgotten or suppressed as children because we were told to behave a certain way. Or better yet, they are the parts of ourselves we've yet to discover, waiting for us to explore and awaken to them. What you'll find in these pages is a spiritual exploration of the energy of the Divine Feminine and yourself.

I found the archetypes at the beginning of my motherhood. I had two babies in the span of thirteen months and found myself knee-deep in diapers, feedings, and nap schedules, completely lost in my new identity. I had thrown myself full force into my new role as a mother and lost all the other parts of who I was. I found myself in a bit of an identity crisis. By exploring and reading the different archetypes of the goddesses, I was able to reclaim those lost parts of myself as well as find new ones. I was able to work with and heal the Warrior I knew was within me. I was able to tap into the Priestess, my mystical side, and integrate much-needed spiritual practices into my daily life that had been missing for over a decade. I learned how to accept the Dark Goddess, the full force of my being, and I no longer feel ashamed for being emotional.

The world we grew up in is no longer; it's shifting, and there is a call for change. We are answering a call to live closer to our truth, to be authentic. Transparency is more valued than it's ever been. However, I don't believe anything can change until we truly understand ourselves on a deep, intimate level, until we are fully honest about who we are. We must come face-to-face with our truth, our traumas, wounds, and shadows and heal them on a deep soul level. I don't believe we can create a world based on human compassion, equality, and kindness unless we treat ourselves that way first. Heal yourself, and you can then help heal the world.

I believe by connecting with our true essence, finding and speaking our truth, and awakening to our greatest potential, we can heal ourselves, which will then create a ripple effect of healing for our planet. The ways of the power-hungry patriarchy are crumbling, and it's time to bring the feminine back into balance with the masculine. To find this recalibration, we must bring forward the suppressed and hidden archetypes of the Divine Feminine that were previously shunned, cast aside, and tainted, the archetypes that allow women to awaken to their greatest potential. I like to view archetypes as threads, or single strands, that when woven together form the fabric of our being, because we are more than just one thing. We are not just Mothers or Lovers. We can also be Priestesses and Warriors. We are multidimensional beings comprised of several different threads that allow us to be both soft and strong, nurturing and steadfast, wild and calm.

It is time society welcomes back and honors the wisdom of the Crone and accepts the ways of the Witch. It's time we respect the transformative shadows revealed with the Dark Goddess. It's time we become the Wild Woman, liberated and unafraid of our emotions and natural states of living.

This book is meant to help you explore these threads inside of yourself and connect with these archetypes on an energetic soul level. It is meant to help you awaken to the truth of who you are. While there are hundreds of archetypes to choose from, we will be focusing on thirteen, the sacred number of the goddess. With each archetype, you will find there are different goddesses that represent it. You can use this information how you see fit.

If you are familiar with the ways of goddess devotion and feel called to work with a specific deity to open up to the archetypes, please do so; however, it's not required. The stories of the goddesses can help bring a better understanding to the archetypes, which are energetic currents you already know are there, pulsating through you. It's a matter of opening yourself up to them and tuning into the right frequency. This requires you to turn off your mind and drop into your body. Feminine work requires embodiment and a connection to your body wisdom in order to be felt, heard, and awakened. Feminine embodiment is not something you can do with a logical, rational mind. In other words, the way you were taught to learn and examine things must go out the window when it comes to the feminine. This process requires faith, trust, and the ability to surrender to the unknown. It requires movement. Just as the tides of the ocean and phases of the moon are both in constant motion, so is the Divine Feminine.

As we discuss the feminine archetypes throughout this book, you will find a ritual to help you connect to the archetype within. These rituals can be used as a guide. Discern for yourself what feels right and ask yourself how best to connect with the archetype. I've kept these rituals as simple as possible so everyone can have the ability to connect through them. I don't believe you need *things* to connect with the Divine, so you won't find a long list of required herbs, crystals, or material items. These items don't make you spiritual, and you don't need them to help you connect with your divinity. All you need is patience, trust, and an awareness of your mind and body. Some rituals do require pen and paper or a blanket, which are all common household items. The rituals explore the idea of archetypal embodiment and use body movement and wisdom to tap into specific archetypal threads within yourself, providing a way for you to connect with the Divine Feminine.

Consider for a moment the many hats you wear in a day. You go to work in the morning and enter the realm of the boss or employee. When you come home, you are the Mother, checking in on and feeding your children, and at night under the comfort of darkness, you embody the Lover. In each scenario, you behave a little differently. You speak differently to your children or family members than you do to your girlfriends, yet both archetypes are still you. You'll notice as you perform these rituals that they will each feel differently inside your body. With the Warrior, you might have more confidence, carrying yourself a little taller than when you are the fun-loving Maiden. Pay attention to these different energies. Once you are able to pick up on how they feel in your body, you'll be able to call on them in times of need. There is a time and place for each archetype, so by working with their energies through embodiment, we can quickly and easily come back to them.

Each archetype has something different to teach us. Each is a key that unlocks a door to a part of ourselves, the powerful, pure, divine essence of our souls. Each archetype holds gifts and mysteries that are waiting to be explored. By tugging on these threads of our being, we allow ourselves to reclaim our true feminine nature. We learn to remember the beauty of who we are, and we are given the tools to stand firm in our truth.

It's important to know that you can access any of these archetypes at any point in your life. Age is irrelevant. You might feel called to one or two archetypes while reading this book, but perhaps in a year or so, you might feel called to explore others. We are all constantly growing and evolving, so it makes sense that our prominent archetypes will change as well. We will also find archetypes within us that we never thought we would relate to, but I promise you, they are there. They are just waiting for you to start exploring.

In this book, you will also find reflection questions for each archetype that are meant to help you think about how you embody it. Sit with these questions, feel into them, use them as journaling prompts. To open up to the feminine archetypes within yourself, you must be willing to do the work. You must be willing to *feel* into your body and be honest with yourself.

The ways of the Divine Feminine are rising in power, and with this also comes wounds around some of the archetypes. They might be generational or ancestral, but it's up to you to decide what needs your attention and what is blocking you from moving forward. The wounds we will be discussing are around the Mother and Witch archetypes, and we will dive into how best to heal and grow from them. A lot of these wounds are often unconscious until we start exploring them within our psyches. You might meet these topics with some resistance, or you might question and explore why these wounds developed in the first place. Give yourself some grace and be patient as you work with each archetype.

Overall, this book is meant to help you explore potentially hidden parts of yourself, get to know yourself better, and grow on a personal and soul level. It's meant to help you tap into and awaken parts of your being so you may stand firmly in your soul truth. In no way is this meant to be an inclusive list or medical advice. This is for personal exploratory purposes only, for the ways of the mystic are to truly know thyself.

THE MAIDEN

It's fitting we start off with the Maiden, as she is the first archetype represented in the triple goddess (which includes the Maiden, Mother, and Crone). The archetype of the Maiden is one of new beginnings. In the ways of the triple goddess, she is seen as the woman before menstruation or motherhood, but she is so much more than that. She is young and eager, looking to the future with bright eyes. We have all experienced the Maiden at some point in our lives, either when we were young, dreaming of being whisked away by a knight in shining armor, or as we set off on our own path, venturing into the world on our own for the first time. Everything is new and exciting. The Maiden often sees the world through rose-colored glasses, ignorant of any obstacles that might lie ahead. She follows her heart, pursuing whatever it is she wants without restraint. The Maiden might be seen as selfish, but she's living from a soul-based place. She is authentic and manifests her wants and needs. If anything, she is pure, untouched by the pain and suffering of the world.

The Maiden often wants to jump in with both feet, whether it is the beginning of a new relationship, moving to a new home, or starting a new project or job. We often experience the Maiden's magic when we feel butterflies in our stomach and a sense of excitement pulsates through our being. We are hopeful for what is yet to come.

While the Mother is in the stages of nurturing and growing her creation, the Maiden is in preparation mode. She is gathering all of her materials, doing her research, and setting everything up so she can create something new. Think back to a time when you started a new project that lit you up. If it put a smile on your face and you couldn't wait to get started, it was most likely a passion of yours. The Maiden archetype experiences life in this same way, continually investing in her passion projects. Patience might not be a strong suit for someone who is always ready to dive in, but that is what the archetype of the Maiden holds: passion. A passion to begin, passion for a fresh start, passion for bringing something new to life, and passion to go after her dreams and create the life she's always wanted.

I see the Maiden in young virgin goddesses who are untouched by man. Being a virgin goddess has nothing to do with sexuality; it simply means they do not have outside influences dictating their next moves. They are free to make their own decisions. I see the Maiden in the artist, pouring her heart and soul onto the page or canvas. I see the Maiden manifest herself in the young activist, who is eager to stand up for injustices. The Maiden goes after her passions, regardless of what others tell her to do. The Maiden archetype is a necessary one and one we will meet many times throughout life. She is not just for the young or the women without children; she is for anyone who is starting something new. The triple goddess represents the continual spiral of life. We enter the Maiden stage in the beginning, before we nurture our creation during the time of the Mother; then we release our creation as we enter the Crone phase. We are constantly finding ourselves, entering and leaving each stage multiple times throughout our lives.

Women who find themselves stuck in the Mother or Crone phases of life can benefit from becoming reacquainted with the Maiden, for she can help us tap back into the joy of playful living. She is an archetype filled with curiosity, wanting to explore uncharted territory. She brings with her a fresh breath of life, helping us break up our old routines, play, and have fun. Play is not just for children. It allows us to experience freedom, bliss, and creativity and to release our inhibitions. Play allows us to explore in an unstructured way. We learn to relax and go with the flow as we enter the Maiden phase. I encourage any woman who is stuck in a routine of obligations and masculine energy, constantly checking off her endless to-do lists, to tap into the energy of the Maiden, because we aren't just meant to "do" life; we are meant to experience it and live it.

The Maiden can offer us a lot of gifts. She reminds us of a time when life was easier, simpler, and anything seemed possible. The Maiden teaches us to be hopeful, that no matter where we find ourselves in life, we can always start again. We are never too old to embody the Maiden. She helps us fall back in love with life, pursue our passions, follow our dreams, and above all else remain true to who we are.

EMBODYING THE MAIDEN

You can best embody the Maiden by doing something fun or unexpected. Invite play into your life by dressing up in costume, making up a silly song or story with your children, having a solo dance party, or gathering up a group of friends to play board games or charades. Allow yourself to get creative. Start a new project, but not just any project—something that makes you giddy like a schoolgirl. Do something that fuels the flames of your inner fire. Breathe fresh life into the way you live. When was the last time you smiled from ear to ear for something so simple? Embody the Maiden by releasing a bit of structure in your life. Plan a girls' trip. Allow yourself to daydream. Pick up an old, abandoned hobby, something you did or were interested in as an adolescent. Create for the sake of creating.

Life is not meant to be lived in a linear fashion. We think once we grow up, go to school, get married, etc. that we are just checking off boxes as we go down the line. But the truth is we are cyclical beings. We structure our lives around the seasons, going in and out of different phases. Life is a spiral, a dance, moving us up and down, left to right. The pendulum is constantly swinging. After the Crone comes the Maiden once again. We aren't meant to live in just one phase. Make sure you find some time to truly embody the Maiden and get excited about life again. Do something for the simple fact that it brings you joy. That is the gift of the Maiden.

SHADOW ASPECTS OF THE MAIDEN

With every archetype, there are also shadow aspects that might be seen as weaknesses or shortcomings of the archetype itself. The Maiden's shadow is revealed in those who remain stuck in this phase. This archetype is meant to be a natural progression toward the Mother; we are not meant to stay in the Maiden phase forever. She is one of growth, a new beginning to something. Women stuck in the Maiden archetype stunt their growth. They are unwilling to take responsibility for their creations. They'd rather play and have fun than take action and bring their creation to life. There comes a point where daydreams must take root in reality, otherwise it's just a form of escape.

We need to take the steps necessary to bring our creation out into the world. We can't sit idly, hoping someone else will do it for us. If you find yourself waiting or not taking action on what it is you want in life, ask yourself why. What is stopping you? Are you in the shadow aspect of the Maiden? Are you avoiding the responsibility and natural growth required to become the Mother?

MAIDEN
REFLECTION QUESTIONS

_____

○ When was the last time you embodied the Maiden archetype?

○ When was the last time you felt excited about life?

○ Is there something you've been wanting to create and bring into the world?

○ What projects are you currently working on?

○ What piques your curiosity? When was the last time you explored that?

○ How does the Maiden want to be expressed through you?

○ How can you invite more play into your life?

○ What is something you're passionate about doing? What gets you excited?

○ How can you make more time to do the things that bring you joy?

GODDESSES TO WORK WITH
THAT EMBODY THE MAIDEN

O Artemis:
Greek goddess of the hunt and the moon

O Diana:
Roman goddess of the hunt and the moon

O Athena:
Greek goddess of war, crafts, and wisdom

O Persephone (prior to her abduction):
Greek goddess of spring

O Ostara:
Germanic goddess of spring

O Uzume:
Shinto goddess of happiness and dancing

MAIDEN
RITUAL

The Maiden is all about having fun, playing, laughing, and being free. She is young at heart. When was the last time you let yourself just be? When was the last time you let yourself play? To connect with the Maiden, you are going to want to block out a chunk of uninterrupted time. Seriously, put your phone away and take the afternoon to yourself. Go to a park or somewhere outdoors (whether rain or shine), take a walk, and allow yourself to wander and explore. Go without a plan in mind. Allow yourself to get a little lost, allow your intuition to guide you. Splash in the puddles, sink your toes into the sand, or create art out of things you pick up in nature (sticks, stones, leaves).

If you're unable to go outdoors, pick up an activity you used to love as a child. Grab some colored pencils and color, finger paint, sing with a hairbrush as your microphone, dress up in costume and have an impromptu dance party. Whatever you choose to do, allow it to unfold naturally without a plan or destination in mind. Allow yourself to connect with your inner artist. The energy of the Divine Feminine is free-flowing, so allow her to move however she chooses. Allow yourself to create and have fun. Be present in the moment. Turn off all distractions and allow yourself to surrender to the moment. See where it takes you. See what you end up creating. You don't have to let others see what you are creating. Let this be just for you. Let this be a time of reconnection. Reconnect with your inner child. Reconnect with an old hobby. Or finally find the time to try something new you've been wanting to explore. Spend this time reconnecting with your heart and soul.

THE WILD WOMAN

The archetype of the Wild Woman has gained popularity in recent years, mostly due to the book *Women Who Run with the Wolves* by Dr. Clarissa Pinkola Estés, in which she dives into myths and folklore examining the Wild Woman archetype. The Wild Woman archetype is one I urge every woman to connect with, as it requires the highest level of body wisdom. The Wild Woman is an archetype you must feel in your body to adequately embody and explore it.

Growing up, most girls are taught to be the "good girl," to follow the rules and do what's expected of them to be rewarded. Women have long been suppressed under patriarchal rule. They were told to keep quiet, to not draw attention to themselves, to not stray too far outside the lines, to be modest, play by the rules of society, and fit inside cultural norms. The Wild Woman is the exact opposite. To truly embrace your Wild Woman within, you must go against everything you've likely been taught. You must go against societal norms, play by your own rules, and do as you please. The Wild Woman is a free spirit, carving her own path in the world, a path many don't understand because, again, it's not "the norm." But that is the beauty of the archetype: she goes where she feels called. She trusts her intuition and her body above all else, because she recognizes the wisdom it carries.

For centuries, men have wanted to suppress the Wild Woman, for she is untamed. She is powerful and passionate, and they often fear what they can't control. To be a woman is to experience raw emotions, highs and lows and everything in between. It's our greatest strength and one we've been ridiculed for throughout history. The very essence of feminine energy is Shakti, or kundalini energy, a serpentine life force energy that snakes its way where it pleases, for it cannot be contained, nor is it supposed to be. This very same energy can be found throughout Mother Nature in hurricanes, earthquakes, tornadoes, the spring breeze, flowers in bloom, and gently flowing rivers. The nature of feminine energy is both creation and destruction, and the Wild Woman embodies it all, because she is in touch with her truth. She allows her emotions to emerge and pass naturally. She experiences freedom without boundaries, owning the fullness of her complexity. She does not apologize for how she lives her life.

The Wild Woman is instinctual, connected to natural rhythms and cycles. Something happens to us when we begin to open up to this archetype, for we also become reacquainted with the land around us. To be in sync with your Wild Woman within, you must also be in sync with the nature that surrounds you. Our modern world has become so far removed from nature, from living in temperature-controlled rooms to having the ability to get anything delivered to our doorstep with the push of a button. It takes the guesswork and mystery out of life. By living our lives indoors, we miss so many opportunities to change our fate, make a new friend, or take a new path. We miss all of these opportunities because we prefer comfort; we are creatures of habit. This is why embodying the Wild Woman is so important and necessary for the modern woman. We've become so far removed from nature in our modern setting that to awaken the Wild Woman means to reconnect with Mother Nature, to connect with the nature within us. Mother Nature does not need humans to carry on. We've seen this firsthand in places that humans have long ago abandoned. Roots break through concrete, and vines snake up and entangle long-abandoned buildings. Her waters will run clear once we stop passing through. Mother Nature depends on no one, and neither does the Wild Woman.

I believe women are turning more and more to the Wild Woman within to make up for and heal past ancestral traumas that have been inflicted upon women in general, women who were sold into slavery and sex work, women who were beaten for being disobedient or were told they brought shame upon their families. Women have had to endure too much pain for too long. No longer does a woman need to depend on a man to define her worth. We have been given back our rights to own land and to vote. By embracing the Wild Woman, we are reclaiming all that was not afforded to our ancestors.

Look back into your maternal blood line. How much suffering did the women in your family have to endure? How often were they told how to behave, dress, and live their lives? You probably don't have to go too far back into your family tree to find a woman who was constrained, unable to live life on her terms, sacrificing her way of living, her divine rights, and her very essence to conform to the lives of others. You get to put a stop to that pattern now by embracing the wildness within you. By returning to the land and reconnecting with Mother Nature as well as with your internal nature, you will be able to heal. You will be able to connect to the natural rhythms and cycles of life. You will be able to heal your maternal ancestral lineage.

Modern Western culture places too much emphasis on getting things done. There are always things to do. When people ask us how we are, we habitually reply, "Busy," because there doesn't seem to be an alternative. We fill our days with obligation after obligation, but I ask you, what kind of life is that? What kind of life is it to serve the system rather than yourself? We are in a time when we are co-creating a new collective consciousness, one that values and honors the Divine Feminine and her way of being. While there are strengths and weaknesses of both the masculine and feminine, both are necessary. The masculine can help us get things done and go after our dreams. It can hold space for us and provide us with stability, but it's the feminine, the act of creation, that plants the seed of possibility in the first place.

Connecting with your inner Wild Woman requires an ability to drop out of the logical mind and into the intuitive wisdom of the body. The Wild Woman moves based on instinct. She connects to the ancient, primal wisdom that is buried within her. It's something you must experience for yourself, something only you can unlock the doors to. When you discover the Wild Woman, it's like coming home to yourself. All the intuitive knowledge you need resides in your body. The world wants scientific evidence, facts, proof, and data, but that is not the way of the Wild Woman.

Embodying the Wild Woman takes courage to open yourself to the vastness that is the human experience. This archetype feels it all: the highs and the lows, the pain and the pleasure. To be able to really experience one, you must have the other. Only after times of sadness can you really be grateful for times of happiness. It's only after the rainstorm that you get to experience the rainbow. That is the way of the Wild Woman; she embraces it all. She does not fear the judgment of others because she is living for herself. She does not require validation. Yes, she lives with unpredictability, but she remains true to herself through it all.

It's funny calling this archetype "wild" because while it seems so far from society's perfectly constructed boxes, it's really just about reconnecting with our true nature. Being a Wild Woman does not mean you must remove yourself from society; it simply means you should feel and experience life through more than just your rational mind. To embrace this archetype, you must honor the wisdom of Mother Nature, for she is your mentor and source of nourishment. When we turn back toward nature, we find inspiration, a temple, medicine, and healing. The Wild Woman sees the breeze as her mother's caress, the rain as her mother's tears, and tornadoes as her mother's warnings. She knows this because she feels them too. When she becomes overwhelmed, she takes to the woods, rivers, or mountains to find clarity and solitude, because it's in those quiet moments that she can finally hear her own voice. She cannot be tamed, because those who taste the freedom of the wild never leave.

The women who most need to explore their Wild Woman are the women who feel trapped, helpless, or lost. If you find yourself going about your life feeling numb and like you can no longer hear the voice of your intuition, go outside. Reconnect with not only Mother Nature but *your* nature. When life and creativity seem to have left you, tap back into passion, vibrancy, and your personal brand of soul food. Bring meaning and value back to your life. The Wild Woman knows the way; she knows where to look and where to turn to ignite that spark of passion once again. It only requires you to embrace stillness and silence. You'll feel her bubbling up within you, snaking her way through and crawling her way out. Honor your body and its wisdom, and it will grant you many gifts. Fill your soul with nourishment, finding meaning and purpose in your life. The Wild Woman knows which path to take. Give in to your natural cycles, honor your patterns, and start incorporating more time for dance, play, and self-expression. Unleash your creative nature. Don't make excuses here. Now is not the time for "I don't have time," "I'm not creative," or "I don't know where to begin." Yes, you do; your body knows.

EMBODYING THE WILD WOMAN

To fully experience the Wild Woman, you must first cultivate self-awareness. This is required to determine when you are letting your logical mind control your emotions rather than letting your body take the lead. Think head versus heart. But it's not just your heart that feels; it's your gut, your womb, your fingers and toes. Emotions are a part of the human experience. We are not immune to any of them, as much as we wish we could be. Don't be fooled by the picture-perfect lives you see online. Everyone suffers, and everyone experiences joy. That is the way of life, after all.

To embody the Wild Woman, you must first allow your emotions to arise. Anything you've been feeling or holding on to, let it come up and out of you. It's never healthy to push down our emotions or allow them to fester and create deep-seated wounds that are patiently waiting to attack when we least expect it. We all must learn to express our emotions in a healthy way and acknowledge them as part of the human experience instead of taking them out on our family, friends, or the random store clerk. If you're angry and want to punch something, punch a pillow, scream, rage, allow your body to contort and contract, and squeeze it all out of you, every last drop. If you're sad, cry, wail, or curl up into a ball. If you're joyous, jump, scream, and stamp your feet in excitement. Anything is allowed. Emotions are allowed. Allow yourself to experience and *feel* it all. Even Mother Nature expresses her emotions freely, so you are allowed to as well.

Once you have sat with all of your feelings and have cultivated the emotional awareness and freedom to express them, you may now slowly start to see the Wild Woman seep into your life. You might spend more time outdoors on nature walks or bring more earth elements indoors. You might dress in more relaxed, free-flowing clothes, and you might see yourself interacting with nature and animals in a completely new way.

Recognize which animals you are drawn to, which plants speak to you, and which ones you tend to favor. Do some research on the meaning and medicinal/healing properties of those plants.

Live your life in a less structured way. Put more free time into your schedule. Allow yourself to explore more. Go where you are drawn to. Do what feels right in any given moment. Use self-awareness to see how your body reacts to certain situations, conversations, and places. Recognize when your body says yes versus when it says no. Practice intuitive eating. Learn to listen to and trust your body and give in to where it wants you to go. Embracing the Wild Woman means remembering your connection to the natural world, breaking free from the systems and structures imposed on you from an early age, and prioritizing freedom while remaining grounded.

SHADOW ASPECTS OF THE WILD WOMAN

To embody the Wild Woman, you must be able to feel, be, and experience. Her ways are free-flowing. However, too much of anything can swing the pendulum too far to one side, and you must be careful to bring it back into balance. The Wild Woman archetype is feminine energy at its root. You can very easily get lost in this energy; I know firsthand the lures of the feminine. It feels good to just be, to create with abandon and let everything come to be. Yet, when we are not balancing our feminine and masculine energies, we become off balance. If you are too much in a free-flowing state or are too receptive, you might find it hard to get things done. The masculine provides us with the structure and activity to turn our creations into reality. It provides stability and purpose in our lives. Masculine energy gives us clarity on the direction of our lives. When we balance these two energies, we are able to focus more on our goals and dreams and the steps needed to obtain them, rather than just letting them dance across our imaginations.

In addition, when working with the Wild Woman, it's common to be in a constant state of rage—rage for the containment and domestication our current society teaches women to embrace, and rage for all the times you didn't trust your intuition. Anger is a common emotion, and the desire to be free triggers us to think of all the times we felt caged and unable to express ourselves. The key here is to work through the anger in a healthy way. There is a fine line between letting emotions move through you and allowing them to consume you whole. Don't get stuck in this anger. Don't let anger be the driving force behind what you choose to do or say. Work through those feelings and align with the highest expression of the Wild Woman, the one who does and says all things with love, the one who can acknowledge that her feelings are a part of the human experience. She allows herself to sit with these feelings, but she also chooses to release them once they've served their purpose.

Lastly, the Wild Woman's main desire is to be free to express herself, live life on her terms, and simply be herself. She values her independence and does not want anything or anyone to tie her down, for that would indicate a form of control over her that she's tried so hard to avoid. But by setting these boundaries, she may keep others at a safe distance, seeming unapproachable to outsiders. And while personal boundaries are always important, you must not let the drive for independence cause you to push others away. Independence is not the same as isolation.

WILD WOMAN
REFLECTION QUESTIONS

○ When was the last time you allowed yourself to feel all of your emotions without suppressing them?

○ How easy is it for you to turn off your mind and drop into your body?

○ What is your relationship with nature?

○ When was the last time you danced?

○ Do you currently keep track of your natural cycles (menstruation, mood, cravings, etc.)?

○ Do you feel that you must live up to the "good girl" image? If so, why?

○ Do you consider yourself instinctual?

○ How can you add more time for uninhibited self-expression to your routine?

GODDESSES TO WORK WITH
THAT EMBODY THE WILD WOMAN

_0_ Artemis:

Greek goddess of the hunt and the moon

_0_ Diana:

Roman goddess of the hunt and the moon

_0_ Kali:

Hindu goddess of time, death, and destruction

_0_ Pele:

Hawaiian goddess of volcanos

_0_ Devana:

Slavic goddess of the wild and the hunt

_0_ Epona:

Celtic goddess of the Earth and horses

WILD WOMAN
RITUAL

The way of the Wild Woman is embodiment, so for this ritual, you will be dropping into your body. It's preferred that you complete this ritual outdoors, but I understand that not all of us have access to a safe space outside where we can be alone.

For this ritual, start by taking a walk outdoors and gathering anything that calls to you, such as sticks, pinecones, flowers, or rocks. Then, take your treasures and create a circle around you. If you have a small drum, bring it with you. Otherwise, you can easily make one out of a coffee can or a large bowl, or you can simply tap on your legs. When you feel ready, begin drumming in the middle of your circle. Start making music with your hands and your body. Sink into the drum beats. Feel the rhythm as it swells around you. Close your eyes and let your body move how it feels called to move. Give yourself permission to move however you want to. Don't think about whether you are doing it "right" or not. Don't worry about what you look like doing this. This isn't about being sexy or coordinated; it's about allowing the energy to arise within and flow through you. It's about dropping into the ancient wisdom held within your body. Give yourself time for this ritual, at least an hour uninterrupted, so you can deepen the energy.

If you're really having trouble creating your own music, find some shamanic drumming tracks online and play them on a portable speaker. Feel the music, relax your body, and sway your hips; move in whatever way you feel called to.

For this ritual, we are dropping in and dancing. We are dancing to unleash our Wild Woman and honor the goddess of the wilderness. Move as the Wild Woman you are. Don't suppress yourself here. This is a no-judgment zone. If you feel called, invite a goddess to dance with you and help you open up to the inner wilderness that's yearning to be explored. We are adventurers ready for our quest. We dance to feel our bodies move, let our hair down, let our breasts bounce and our hips rock back and forth, and feel the Shakti wind her way up and around our bodies as we surrender to the Divine. We move and dance to open our bodies energetically and better open ourselves up to the Divine. Surrender to the goddess. Ask for wisdom and guidance. Dance naked, dance under the stars, dance on top of a mountain, dance however and wherever you feel called to, surrendering to the flow and reclaiming your inner Wild Woman. Most importantly, remember to feel and experience it all.

THE WARRIOR

The Warrior is one of the most easily recognizable archetypes in this book. On first thought, we think of the Warrior as a fighter, one preparing for battle or seeking justice. While all of this may be true to a degree, the feminine Warrior is so much more complex than what first meets the eye. At some point in our lives, we have had to learn how to stand up for ourselves, whether to a bully, a family member, or a colleague; this is what it means to tap into the Warrior. It's important here to distinguish between the masculine version of the Warrior archetype and the feminine.

The masculine Warrior archetype very much exudes physical strength, the solider ready for battle, suiting up to fight for what they believe in. Everyone has both masculine and feminine energy within them, so we can very much be describing a man or a woman within these archetypes. I'm not discussing gender here but rather the different traits of masculine and feminine energies. The feminine Warrior deals more with an internal struggle. We are each fighting our own battle, whether it be depression, anxiety, or some other internal struggle we must prepare ourselves to face. There is a quiet strength and an ability to be vulnerable with this version of the archetype. Sometimes vulnerability and having the ability to speak our truth is our greatest strength.

A Warrior is fierce. She is not a victim. She is one who fights back. She speaks up when she sees injustices. The Warrior is powerful and knows how to persevere. We see this archetype shine through in activists, female officers, and bosses. Not all Warriors are outspoken, though. She doesn't always have to shout and spread her message for all to hear; there are quiet Warriors too. Single moms, athletes, and those battling severe or silent illnesses are also Warriors. There is an inner strength there that not everyone can see. Don't confuse this archetype with that of a solider on the battlefield. The feminine Warrior doesn't need to physically fight. In fact, she will do everything in her power to avoid it, using diplomacy and strategy to overcome her obstacles.

The Warrior archetype must carry two very important tools with her to succeed in battle. First, she must have a sword to cut away the falsehoods and lies that are being told, whether by herself or someone else. We encounter several thousand messages in a day, whether we are conscious of it or not. It's up to us to determine what rings true for us as an individual, so the Warrior needs this figurative sword to protect herself from lies. It allows her to get to the truth of the issue. It cuts away at everything that comes her way, whether it's ill advice from loved ones, advertisements selling the next miracle cream, or her ego flaring up and telling her to hide or play it safe. The Warrior knows the way to the truth, and when you embody this archetype, your sword will be the best offensive tool you'll have. Consider it a soul litmus test of sorts.

The next tool a Warrior must have is a shield to block and defend her from any negativity coming her way, whether it's an angry individual, manipulative or narcissistic energy, or an energetic vampire trying to suck away her optimism. If you identify as an empath or someone who is highly sensitive, the Warrior with her shield is an extremely important archetype for you to tap into. The Warrior's shield can help you energetically block anything that does not serve you. It prevents you from getting carried away into someone else's energy. Leaving interactions with the same energetic vibrations they started with is paramount for sensitives. Just like the Warrior going into battle, it's important to carry your shield at all times.

As an empath myself, I know how difficult it can be sometimes to learn how to stop ourselves from getting mixed up in someone's emotions, especially if it's someone we love. You want to be there for them, you feel their pain, and you want to lend support, but you must learn not to carry that burden as your own. The shield helps protect you from all incoming attacks on both an energetic and psychic level. The Warrior helps us establish boundaries in our lives so we aren't taken advantage of by others. She helps us say no with confidence and strength.

We should summon the Warrior when we need courage to face a difficult decision. The Warrior lends us her strength, power, and confidence to see anything through. She reminds us of our self-worth and the need to protect it at all costs. She is the archetype that seeks justice; she wants to protect herself and others, and she stands firmly in her truth. Just thinking about the Warrior archetype makes me sit up a little straighter and carry myself a little taller. Try standing in a superhero pose with your feet planted slightly apart, your hands on your hips, and your chin pointing slightly upward and tell me you don't feel more confident and capable of tackling your day.

Not only do you want to tap into your inner Warrior if you are an empath who struggles to maintain boundaries in your life, but you also want to tap into this archetype if you need help persevering toward your goals. The Warrior is like an endurance athlete. No matter what battles you face, she reminds you of the reason why you are fighting in the first place. She connects you with your soul's truth, and once you have that, you will feel unstoppable. The Warrior empowers us to keep going.

The Warrior also needs to protect her mind from negative thoughts, self-doubts, and false beliefs. The Warrior doesn't worry about trying to impress others; she has left her ego at the door. She isn't being strong for attention or praise; rather, she is strong because her truth needs her to be. The divine Warrior comes from a place of soul alignment. She is in touch with her divinity and intuition and allows them to guide her in all her endeavors. The feminine Warrior must be aligned in her heart and mind. This is an action-oriented archetype, and if she is aligned with her soul truth and with her heart, she must take action and act in accordance with it. She reminds us that we can't believe one thing and then behave differently. The Warrior must compassionately fight battles (both internal and external) based on her set of values and beliefs.

EMBODYING THE WARRIOR

To fully step into the most divine expression of the Warrior, you must first align with your soul's truth. What beliefs do you carry at your core that you cannot waver from? Embodying the Warrior means standing firmly in your truth and recognizing that it is yours alone. We are not here to change each other's minds. Someone else's truth will be different from yours, and that's OK. Become clear on what your truth is and use your sword to cut away everything else. Cut away the ego, fears, doubts, lies, or old programming you've been holding on to. To be a Warrior, you must not allow others to easily sway or manipulate you. You must stand tall. You must be confident. You must possess a deep sense of faith in yourself and honor the feminine wisdom you carry. The Warrior does not react to situations, but rather takes her time to respond.

What does it feel like to be strong and confident? Feel it in your body, deep down in your bones. Sit with this energy and let it emanate out of you and surround you. Know that you are capable of extraordinary things. You have everything you could ever need. You carry truth and wisdom within you. You are a divine Warrior; have no doubt about that. Whatever battles you face, problems you must deal with, obstacles that are thrown your way, or injustices you must correct, you carry with you the energy and determination to see them through. You have the will and strength to push on undaunted. No demon or hardship will last long while you carry the sword of truth and shield of protection. Rise up. Protect, defend, and, most of all, love.

SHADOW ASPECTS OF THE WARRIOR

There is a fine line one must walk between the shadow and light aspects of this archetype. If you cross over into the shadow side, you might be fighting for all the wrong reasons. Those stuck in the shadow aspects of this archetype are typically manipulative, aggressive, and vengeful. They are fighting in a way that is not soul-aligned but more out of fear. Their ego tends to be the driver in these circumstances, and they are missing the heart-mind connection. They might be competitive, cold, or ruthless, or they might have a hard time accepting help from others. The shadow aspect of the Warrior shows up in the woman who abandons her moral and ethical principles to obtain her preferred outcome. At what cost does it take to win your battles? Pay attention to where you draw the line when it comes to obtaining success. Be sure you are aligned with your soul's truth before heading off into battle.

The Warrior wants what is best for everyone. It's time for women to stop competing against one another and instead to encourage and support one another. We are all in this journey of life together. There are plenty of resources to go around, and there is no need to be competitive and tear one another down. That is not the way of the heart-centered feminine Warrior. Yes, she must be strong, confident, and have the ability to persevere, but she can also be vulnerable and soft while staying true to herself and her beliefs. As I mentioned before, this is one of the easiest archetypes to recognize, but there is so much more to her than meets the eye. The feminine Warrior has depth, soul, and character. She's not just about fighting battles but rather doing it in a way that allows you to stand firm and speak your truth.

WARRIOR
REFLECTION QUESTIONS

O Do you find it difficult to set boundaries for yourself?

O Would you consider yourself an empath or a highly sensitive person? If so, do you have trouble refraining from taking on other people's emotions or problems?

O When do you feel most strong or confident?

O When in your life have you had to stand up for yourself or others?

O Do you find it easy to speak up against injustices? If not, what holds you back from doing so?

O When you think of the Warrior archetype, what comes to mind for you? What does she feel like in your body?

GODDESSES TO WORK WITH
THAT EMBODY THE WARRIOR

0 Kali:
Hindu goddess of time, death, and destruction

0 Athena:
Greek goddess of war, wisdom, and crafts

0 Freyja:
Norse goddess of war and love

0 Morrigan:
Celtic goddess of battle, death, and prophecy

0 Durga:
Hindu warrior goddess

0 Sekhmet:
Egyptian goddess of war and healing

0 Pele:
Hawaiian goddess of volcanos

0 Themis:
Titan goddess of divine law and order

WARRIOR
RITUAL

———

To fully step into our inner Warrior, we must prepare for (metaphorical) battle. I want you to dress up in your most powerful outfit, whether that looks like a power suit, a leather jacket, or some dramatic heels. Notice how your energy shifts as you put on your armor. It should make you stand up taller and feel stronger and more confident.

To complement the powerful outfit, we must also speak our truth. To do so, it's important to open up our throat chakra. Some easy ways to do this are to sing loudly or scream. Is there a certain situation that is infuriating you, and do you feel like you can't speak out? Use this ritual to channel that energy. Scream, yell, or hit a pillow if you need to. Get that energy out! It's only going to get worse if you bottle it up and hold on to it. Maybe there is a situation at work or in your relationship that you feel powerless in. Channel that energy and use it to emote and bring your voice back. This will help open up your throat chakra. The next time you find yourself in the same situation, you will be better equipped to handle it. You will be able to speak up and stand in your truth, because now you've practiced doing so.

Now that you are dressed in your "Warrior suit," I want you to imagine yourself preparing for battle. First, create an energetic field around yourself. Picture a white light at the top of your head and pull this down and around you to encompass your entire body. This is your shield. This energetic field is to protect you from other people's energy. This isn't something to keep you contained; it's something designed to keep others out. The energy you want to exude outward can leave, but nothing can come inside unless you want it to. Imagine it as a one-way door.

Next, we must create our energetic sword. Envision your hand wrapping around the sheath of an invisible sword. Feel its weight in your hands. This sword is for cutting through all the noise and opinions being thrown at you throughout the day. Slay the dragons that try to attack you and see them fall to the ground. Don't let others' opinions or words impact you. Your sword will cut right through them and only allow the truth to be revealed.

Lastly, we must have a helmet. If you've included a hat as part of your Warrior suit, perfect! This can act as your helmet. If a hat is not part of your Warrior suit, then I recommend you find some special headgear, whether it's a headband, hair clip, or another accessory you can adorn your hair or head with. Why not add some extra bling to your Warrior outfit? It doesn't have to be huge, but imagine placing it on top of your head to create a force field around you and your mind. You can cleanse your accessory before placing it on your head, asking it to only allow good thoughts to enter your mind. Ask it to protect you from negative thoughts, self-doubt, criticism, and false beliefs. When you see or feel it throughout the day, you will be reminded of its purpose.

I would love to see your Warrior outfit! Post a picture of yourself on social media using #warriorsuit. You might just inspire another woman to embrace her inner Warrior! In today's world, it's important to come together as women and lift each other up. It's so beautiful to see all of the variations of what makes a woman feel strong and empowered.

THE HUNTRESS

The Huntress might not be the first archetype that comes to mind when you think of the Divine Feminine, but it's a necessary one. The Huntress is an archetype that gets things done. She harnesses her action-oriented masculine energy and uses it to achieve her heart's desires. The Huntress is incredibly focused and goal driven. When she sets her sights on something, she has unwavering determination to complete or achieve it. The Huntress has an inner spirit that cannot be subdued; she is her own person. She draws on her inner source of strength and power to survive. You'll never see her playing the victim. Her aim is true as she looks ahead to the future.

A hunter is someone with a goal in mind, stalking their prey and waiting for an opportune time to strike. As such, the Huntress knows that waiting is sometimes a part of the game, which can be frustrating, since patience is a concept we are losing in our modern society. In today's world, we don't do nearly as much hunting or gathering as we used to in pre-industrialization times, but regardless, the Huntress is still very much alive in us all. The Huntress is goal driven; she seeks to perform well and follow through until the very end, whether in her career or her personal life. She is always striving for more—to be better, to *do* better—and she is far from lazy. The Huntress is very much connected to her instinctual self and effortlessly navigates through corporations, charity work, and her home. She has her sights set on a prize, whether it's a prominent leadership role at work or simply a celebratory dinner after running a marathon. It doesn't matter what your end goal is, but if you have one, consider yourself on the hunt to obtain it. As a Huntress, you don't care how long it takes or what obstacles you must overcome. You are determined to rise to the top, do your best, and claim your prize.

A Huntress also needs to take time to prepare. She needs to study the way of her prey, or in modern context, she needs to figure out the steps to obtain her goal. A Huntress can't just go out into the world and hope to capture her prey. She must pack up her bow and arrow, put on the proper attire, and know where she needs to look to make her kill. Preparation is required for any goal. What tools are you going to need? How much research will you do beforehand? What is your plan after you hit your target?

Being a Huntress requires patience. Most goals will not be achieved overnight. A Huntress recognizes that she might have to wait for some time before the deer crosses her path, for there is a divine timing for everything. You have a greater chance of achieving your goal if you know the steps you are going to take to get there. Break it down and take it one step at a time. Once you know those action steps, you must be disciplined enough to stay on course and determined enough to see it through. Nothing that is currently in existence would be here today if the creator behind it decided to give up. If you embody the Huntress, you'll soon be achieving your goals!

Imagine being so committed to your goal that no one could sway you; your tunnel vision makes your goal your main priority. You may work in a fever, creating, reviewing, and proposing new ideas, or you may follow the pre-paved steps to your success. This is what it's like to embody the Huntress. It's a devotion like no other, because failing is not an option. Deep within your bones, you know you can and will meet your goal. Sometimes the road is longer than you imagined; there may be many detours, but the end goal never changes. Every choice you make is with the purpose of seeing your endeavors through. The commitment and determination of the Huntress is unmatched.

People may try to talk you out of it or make excuses for you by saying, "It's OK if you don't make it" or "If you don't have expectations, you'll never be disappointed." Others will tell you it's not the destination but the journey. For the Huntress, it's all of it, the journey *and* the destination. Only you can see the prize at the end. Only you will know what it means to truly live out your dreams. The Huntress keeps us on our life's path. There is a drive and a purpose to everything she does. The myriad of choices you make all amount to the vision you hold.

We need the Huntress in our lives during moments when the detours are too much, the pressure is too great, and our faith starts to waver. We can call on the Huntress to remind us of our vision and why we are fighting and paving the way forward in the first place. We need the Huntress to help us embody the same determination and grit we had when we first started out on our path. The Huntress lives in the activist who endlessly campaigns for a better world. She's seen in the young woman going after her lifelong dream. She lives in the entrepreneur who creates her own path in the world. The Huntress is the propulsion forward. This archetype might also be one of the easiest to embody because she requires both the masculine, left-brain, logical mind as well as the feminine, right-brain, instinctual self. She balances these energies within herself and utilizes the strengths of both to achieve new pathways.

Don't let the fear of not obtaining your goal stop you before you even start. Fear can easily stop us in our tracks—fear of not succeeding, fear of getting it wrong, fear of what others will think of us if we set out to do whatever our hearts desire. Fear is our ego's way of keeping us safe. Our ego wants us to blend in and not draw attention to ourselves because if all eyes are on us, we can easily become a target. Yet, the world can't change and grow if we don't have a few rebels and change-makers along the way. This is why it's so important to be connected to what is driving you. Be so connected to your goal and your soul's truth that fear can never get in the way. Sure, you might have doubts along the way, but that is perfectly normal. Doubt and fear are normal human emotions, but be sure not to get so sucked up in them that they keep you from going after your dream.

Being aware of our emotions and thoughts helps us acknowledge those common doubts and fears, sit with them for a moment, and allow them to move on. The best way to move around fear and doubt is to have an accountability partner. Tell someone you trust what you plan on achieving and ask them to check in on you every now and then to see how you're progressing. We should all have someone supporting us and cheering us on. Not only does it help keep us motivated, but having support is something we all need no matter what journey we choose to embark on in life.

EMBODYING THE HUNTRESS

To embody the Huntress, you must actively pursue your goals while remaining faithful to yourself. Trust in divine timing. Set a plan of action in place to see your dreams fulfilled, and never give up hope that they will come to fruition. The Huntress knows there is a time and place for everything. She understands that she is the co-creator of her reality. She has the ability to change and create a new path for herself at any time. She has the ability to make her mark in the world. To embody this archetype, you must have a level of self-discipline, never give up hope, and continuously pursue your heart's desires. Don't let others sway you from achieving your dream. Only you know your truth, and only you know your every want and desire. Go after them and know that you deserve it all. You are worthy of receiving it all. Be unwavering in your pursuit of joy. Embody the feeling of success and constantly hold the vision of your achievement in your mind. Maintain the drive and determination to see it through to the end.

SHADOW ASPECTS OF THE HUNTRESS

The shadow aspect of the Huntress shows itself when someone's goal is to hunt and tear down others instead of protect them. Someone who is fixated on doing things for all the wrong reasons, like for a personal vendetta or revenge, is most likely living in the Huntress's shadow energy. If you are unsure whether you are experiencing the shadow aspect of this archetype, ask yourself if your goal is for the greatest good of all those involved. Are you coming from a place of heartfelt love and service or from fear and anger?

Another shadow of this archetype is found in the inability to let go of control. As the Huntress, you want a specific outcome, but what if the way you obtain that outcome is different from what you originally thought? Remember, the energy of the Divine Feminine is free-flowing; she needs space to move, adapt, and be flexible. Can you be flexible with how you obtain your goal? Can you be open to obtaining even more than what you thought imaginable? It's so important for all of us to have goals, because they give us a purpose in life. They keep us moving forward, growing and developing as individuals. Very rarely are substantial goals obtained easily. There are always unforeseen challenges or roadblocks, and I like to view those challenges as tests from the Universe. Those obstacles we face when going after our goals help us reconfirm our why. We are reminded why we are striving for the goal in the first place, and it makes us be honest with ourselves about how important that goal actually is to us. When it's of significant importance, we are more than determined to win, but we need to have some flexibility in how we win. When we are rigid and set in our ways, we block ourselves from receiving other levels of abundance or support from others. The path may change along the way, but the Huntress always keeps her eye on the target. The Huntress also recognizes that our own plans and dreams may change along the way. She must give herself grace to redirect and reroute those goals, but she never gives up in her pursuit.

HUNTRESS
REFLECTION QUESTIONS

○ What goals are you currently working toward? Do you have a plan in place to help you achieve those goals?

○ Are you open to receiving help from others?

○ Can you be adaptable in the ways in which you obtain your goal?

○ What is your why? *Why* are you going after this goal? What does it mean to you?

○ Do any doubts or fears come up when you think about setting out to accomplish your goal? What are those fears? How can you work past them?

○ Have you shared this dream with anyone? Do you have someone who can hold you accountable?

○ Do you have a lifelong dream but continually find yourself making excuses to not pursue it?

GODDESSES TO WORK WITH
THAT EMBODY THE HUNTRESS

⟋

○ Artemis:

Greek goddess of the hunt and the moon

○ Diana:

Roman goddess of the hunt and the moon

○ Medeina:

Lithuanian goddess of the forest, trees, animals, and the hunt

○ Pinga:

Inuit goddess of the hunt, fertility, and medicine

○ Banka Mundi:

Hindu goddess of the hunt and fertility

HUNTRESS
RITUAL

What is one goal that's been on your bucket list forever? Are you currently working toward a big goal in your life? Perhaps you want to save money to make a big purchase, to plan a trip around the world, or to do something different in your career. Do you have a plan in place to help you achieve that goal? As mentioned, the Huntress is one of the most masculine, action-oriented archetypes I'll discuss in this book. She must have a plan in place. I encourage you to think of a goal you've been wanting to achieve for some time and, with a pen and paper, map out your journey to that goal.

This is more than just a vision board. Sure, you can add pictures along the way, but you need to first decide how long it's going to take you to achieve this goal—one month, one year, five years? Then, you must write down the steps you will take to get there. How you write this down is completely up to you. You could get creative and make an actual bullseye target, with each ring representing a step you'll take. You could add small steps to your calendar each month to remind you of the end goal as you go. Or you could create a list of steps to take in chronological order. It could even look like a treasure map, marking your way to the treasure chest, your end goal.

Whatever you decide, put your plan down in writing, and once that's done, share it with someone. Tell your spouse, your best friend, or anyone else you trust and can depend on to be an accountability partner. Set up reminders each week, or each month, to check in on your progress.

By planning your goals and telling others about your vision, you are signaling to the Divine, the Universe, and God that you are ready to make this your reality. This takes your vision from a daydream to a possibility. Once you have your plan in place, take your first action step. Maybe it's something as simple as making a phone call or sending an email. Whatever it is, take one small step to set the plan in action. Those dreams you've been thinking about are in your mind for a reason. Trust that you are being guided along your journey and picture yourself ultimately achieving those goals.

THE LOVER

The Lover archetype can help open us up to one of the most expansive and universal feelings in the Universe: pure love. It's the part of us that comes through when we fall in love, whether romantically, platonically, or with a newborn baby in our arms. The Lover archetype is within every single being that yearns to be loved, admired, adored, and seen on an intimate level by another. The Lover in us can be so enamored with another human being that we put blinders on and become unable to see anything else in our lives—at least for a short period of time. I would like to examine this archetype through three different lenses, the first being universal/divine/God love, then self-love, and lastly romantic or sexual love. These are all the same unconditional, joy-filled, enrapturing love but viewed from different sources. Because how we view love and open ourselves up to it will vary greatly for all of us, it's important to distinguish between the roles of the Lover in each circumstance.

Whether or not you believe in God, Source, the Divine, or the Universe doesn't matter. There is a universal language we all know, a frequency so high and abundant that we have all experienced it at one point in our lives. It is the language of Earth, of humans, of the Universe, and it flows through all living things. Love might be expressed in different ways and it may look different from person to person, but in our bodies, it's felt in the same way. Love is the stuff of poets, for those of all ages. Love is patient and kind. Love is flowing to you and through you at all hours of the day, whether you are tapped into it or not. We all start at the same point when we come into this world, safe in our mother's womb, attached to a supply of endless and universal love. This love, the love you can tap into from the Universe/God/Divine, is endless and unconditional. You can take a moment right now to tap into it.

Sit with your eyes closed and take a few deep, cleansing breaths. When you are ready to sink into your heart space, place a hand on your heart and as you breathe in, fill your heart with divine love. Notice as your chest starts to rise and your heart starts to swell. Picture a divine golden light coming in through the top of your head, connecting your heart to the heavens above. Down that golden thread of light travels love in abundance.

Unwavering, never-ending, divine, pure love. Sit with this divine love for as long as you need to. Know that you can access this at any time, no matter where you are or what you're dealing with. You can pause, close your eyes, and tap into the abundance of love from the Universe. This is a love like no other—a love so pure, it can overpower anything. The origin of its source is irrelevant because it's universal. It's a love we can all feel, a love meant for all of us, no matter who we are, where we live, or what we believe.

Now that you've spent a few moments tapping into this energy and filling your heart with pure divine love, notice how your mood shifts. Notice the smile that spreads across your lips. Notice how you've shifted into the archetype of the Lover.

The Lover, at its core, wants to give and receive love. The Lover helps us open up to pleasure, joy, and abundance, yet it can also be one of the most difficult archetypes to express. So let's look at the Lover through the lens of self-love, because before we can move on to sharing love with others, we must first learn to love ourselves. If we don't master this foundation, we will seek it elsewhere and ultimately find disappointment. Learning to love ourselves must come first. We need to fill our own cups before we can give love to others. When we choose to see ourselves as beautiful and worthy, we radiate that love, and others can feel it. If we skip this step, we often find ourselves seeking love in others or in outside sources, which can lead to tumultuous relationships with people who don't truly love or respect us. We may feel insecure about our self-worth and cling to people who are toxic to us. We may try to earn people's love or approval by bending over backward to make them happy, when in reality, it's ourselves we should be trying to make happy. You can't pour from an empty cup, so you must learn to love yourself unconditionally, flaws and all. You must learn to honor and respect your body, the very thing that allows you to experience pleasure and joy. You must learn to feel worthy of receiving love, from yourself and then from others.

We can be our own worst critics and can sometimes tear ourselves apart if left with our thoughts for too long. Pay attention to how you speak to yourself during the day. Are you hard on yourself? Do you wish you had reacted in a different way or were more forgiving? Do you give yourself grace for being human and making mistakes? For me personally, the biggest lesson I learned from embodying the Lover was learning how to love myself again. I was a perfectionist and a people pleaser. I wanted to help anybody and everybody, but I did it in a way that drained me. I didn't have boundaries, and I definitely did not take care of myself in the process. I gave everything I had to my family and friends until there was no love left over to give myself. I eventually broke down and started seeing a therapist, who reminded me that I was worthy of love, too. She let me know it was OK to fill my cup; in fact, it was necessary that I did so first. I couldn't see it at the time, but looking back on it now, it was all so toxic. I had a hard time telling people no because I wanted to make them happy, and sometimes that meant I had to suffer. I had to establish boundaries and learn to release the guilt that often went along with turning somebody down.

I learned to set aside time for myself every day. I learned more about myself and what my needs were, and I no longer compromise on my daily self-care time. I also had to learn to stop judging myself. I wanted everything to be perfect all the time, and that by itself is exhausting and unrealistic. It was important for me to learn grace. That is the way of the Lover. You must be able to see yourself for the radiant light you are. It's important you carve out time each day to do things that make you happy and fill your cup. The Lover helps with this by teaching us to go with the flow, surrender to the way of the Divine, and give ourselves a break. It's OK if you don't get everything done, it's OK if you make mistakes, and it's OK if you aren't where you thought you would be at this point in your life. The important thing is to recognize your worthiness for love.

As a society, we must let go of this idea of comparison. We all do it at one point or another. We compare the place we are in our lives to that of our family or friends. We measure our success based on other people's versions of it. We measure our intellect, our weight, our body shape, or our health by that of everyone else. We live in a society that knows how to market to our insecurities, so just when we think we've moved past something, we are hit with it all over again. The Lover teaches us to love ourselves no matter what. Embodying the way of the Lover allows us to detach ourselves from those insecurities because they come from the ego, not the soul. And the way of the Lover is tapping into divine love, pure soul love. Everything is as it should be when you embody the Lover, including you, your thoughts, and your body.

Learn to give from an overflowing cup. What you do to fill your cup is entirely up to you. It could be getting your nails done, having a girls' weekend, finding some alone time, taking a walk, drawing a bath, or establishing boundaries and learning to say no when you want to. Be sure to carve out time to do whatever it is that helps you feel rejuvenated and good about yourself, and remember that self-care is not selfish. When we feel good and take care of ourselves regularly, we tend to be nicer, more giving, and more patient with our fellow beings. Love should never be a conditional thing. When we regularly fill our cups, we have more to give, and as a result, we become better lovers, mothers, friends, and wives. Self-care should include small acts throughout your day to uplift you and to reconnect with yourself.

By filling up our reservoirs with self-love, we are able to love others from the excess. We cannot rely on others to make us happy, for happiness is not something you can obtain; it's something you already possess inside of you. While other people can bring you joy, it's important to not rely on that as your one source of happiness. You must love all parts of yourself to truly find happiness. It's also important to not deny yourself the things that bring you pleasure. Whether it's a piece of chocolate, a glass of wine, gardening, or sex, be sure to include acts of pleasure in your daily routine. Of course, with these, I think everything is better in moderation. If we constantly give ourselves over to pleasure, it won't be as enjoyable as something we only experience every now and then.

The Lover asks you to celebrate every freckle, scar, stretch mark, or gray hair. Self-love is about self-acceptance; loving yourself, including all the flaws, quirks, and shadows. She wants you to embrace yourself as you are in this moment. When we feel comfortable in our skin, when we feel beautiful on the outside as well as the inside, people pick up on that. Our auras radiate that energy, and people are attracted to our confidence and beauty. It's in those moments we can attract others to us. It all starts from within. Once we feel secure in our bodies and have filled our cups, we can then seek out a partner to share ourselves with. Love should flow back and forth equally between partners. There should always be respect, trust, and an open line of honest communication. There is a level of vulnerability required in embodying the Lover and experiencing intimacy, and love as an action should be treated as something sacred.

This brings us to the third and final lens through which we can view love, and that requires sharing it with others, whether platonically or romantically. While divine love and self-love focus on love flowing inward toward the self, this love, the love we give to others, flows outward. It's a love we give freely to other people because we care about them. And yes, we can also add another layer to this and receive love from others. We yearn to be adored, desired, and wanted. We want others to give us love, but we first must heal and awaken this part of the Lover within us before we can truly accomplish the Sacred Union of the Divine Masculine and Feminine.

We have to be willing to receive love. So many of us get hurt by love, by those we consider loved ones, or by those we pour all of our love into only to be hurt, abused, or betrayed. Some find it difficult to let love in, guarding their hearts to prevent pain and heartache. That is why it's so important to open up to the aspects of the Lover that focus on divine love and self-love first. That inward focus helps us slowly open the doors to the Lover before we can be completely vulnerable. There are oftentimes a lot of wounds carried from previous relationships around this aspect of the Lover, wounds we may have inflicted on others we loved or ones that have been inflicted on us.

The archetype of the Lover is very much connected to our root chakra, the place where we feel sexual pleasure, the spot of the body where Shakti resides all coiled up, waiting to be unleashed. As a reminder, these archetypes are just one thread of Shakti energy, one way for us to open up to the ways and mysteries of the Divine Feminine. What I've noticed within myself and with many other women who work with these archetypes and with Shakti, or kundalini energy, is that by tapping into this part of ourselves, healing and accessing our Lover within actually results in a kundalini awakening. A kundalini awakening can only be described as allowing that Shakti energy to flow upward and outward. Imagine a coiled snake residing in your womb, slowly winding its way up and out of your body. When we tap into these archetypes or energetic threads within us, we are awakening parts of the snake.

Suddenly, it may seem like your whole world changes. You start acting differently, carrying yourself differently, choosing healthier foods, engaging with different friends, or listening to different music. You suddenly see the world in a new light because when you awaken Shakti energy within you, you tap into a higher consciousness. You awaken a part of you that has been dormant, and you can tap into a strong inner knowing and universal wisdom that you've long ignored. I mention this here because the Lover is an easy access point to this energy. Sexual energy is an easy portal to tap into to uncoil the snake. For a lot of women, having a kundalini awakening has also greatly improved their sex lives. Their orgasms are more intense, their divine nectar flows more freely, and love is in abundance. Opening up to the Lover within you, healing any traumas you might carry, and purifying yourself with divine love only makes you want to experience it with others. Love is meant to be shared and given freely for all to enjoy. Love is truly what makes the world go round, and when we can get to a place where we can enjoy ourselves and our bodies and find someone who truly respects and honors us, then what else is there to search for?

The Lover wants us to experience pleasure with ourselves and others. It helps us open up to intimacy and allows us to truly desire being seen on a deep level. Romantic relationships should be a partnership, which not only requires honesty and respect but also equal give and take. We all deserve partners who will support us, give a little extra when we need to take a little extra, and vice versa. The Lover wants healthy, consensual connections, and to have that, we must have the self-respect to demand nothing less. The act of sex alone is a sacred right, something that shouldn't be shrugged off as casual. When you enter the realm of the Divine Lover, you are entering into an agreement of sacredness, the unity of masculine and feminine energy. To be clear, I'm not talking about gender here; I'm talking about energy. We all carry both masculine and feminine energy. Think of the masculine as the sacred container, unwavering strength, and the feminine as the movement, the creation of love itself. You can embody the feminine and receive, then switch over to the masculine and give. It's a beautiful dance of the most sacred of unions, the dance of fertility, joy, pleasure, bliss, and love. It's not something that should be taken lightly.

SACRED SEXUALITY

Sacred sexuality starts with us as we discover and explore ourselves and what helps us achieve pleasure. Before we can share our bodies with a partner, we must first get to know ourselves better. We must be comfortable in our skin. We must respect our body temple and be willing to further explore this erotic energy within us. We aren't taught how to be intimate with others. There are no real lessons on the act of sex growing up. What we learn as kids comes from our peers or what we find online. Being intimate with ourselves is natural. It is not something we should be ashamed of. Cultural norms leave most women feeling like they can't measure up to the impossible beauty standards that are constantly being perpetuated. Societal messaging may tell us we have a basic flaw that makes us unattractive and unlovable when that couldn't be further from the truth. It's time we learn to hold our sexual energy as a sacred part of ourselves; it's not something to be repressed. Awakening this primary aspect of ourselves allows us to produce personal power, which can be yielded to create a life that deeply fulfills us.

To truly embrace the Lover, you must open yourself up to pleasure, creation, and the essence of life itself. Our wombs are the epicenter of this power. Our wombs are where we create and sustain life, where we store trauma, where we bleed each month, and where we experience orgasms. To experience the bliss of life, we must be comfortable with and heal our womb space. Over half of all women have never had a real orgasm before, which is a fact that blows my mind. Most women fake it, for reasons I will truly never understand. Faking an orgasm does no one any good. You are doing yourself a disservice. You aren't teaching your partner how to please you, and you aren't opening yourself up to all the pleasure that is meant to be had. I understand that sex may seem taboo for a lot of people. Many of us grew up feeling shame around our bodies and intimacy. We may have a hard time opening ourselves up to that aspect of life, but why? Because it's scary. We fear the power we hold. We fear rejection, betrayal, and so many other things, and we end up storing all of that negativity within our wombs, blocking us from the very thing that can set it all free.

To open yourself up to the many gifts of the Lover, you must open yourself up to these fears and, in doing so, open yourself up to receive. Be willing to experience pleasure in all its forms. Sexual energy is potent and powerful, and when we learn to harness and direct that energy into our creative endeavors, we become truly unstoppable. Keep in mind, you don't need a partner to open up to this energy. This is something you can do all by yourself. It might even be better if you explore these parts of yourself first before sharing them with a partner. A lot of women carry trauma and wounds they didn't even know they had. Orgasms can shake your entire body and knock loose the things you didn't even know you were holding on to. But the more you work with this energy, the more comfortable you will become, the more open you will be to receiving, and the better and more blissful the experience will become.

We often aren't aware of the link between our wombs and our mouths. As a birth doula, I've seen a lot of women struggle with opening themselves up and progressing during birth, and it's often because they are holding all the pain in. They are afraid of emoting what they are going through. But the trick? An open mouth equals an open yoni. I remember in a birthing class one time, the instructor asked all the soon-to-be mothers to make primal sounds—moans, groans, roars, whatever they wanted to. At first, all the mothers looked to their spouses like, *Is she serious?* In the beginning, the moans coming from around the room were soft and muted. They felt awkward and forced. But once all the women joined in and tapped into that raw, primal part of themselves, the roars were truly unleashed. And these were not fake roars but deep, guttural vibrations that hit to the core. Magic happened that day as those women learned to open their throats and give in to the sounds of the Lover. Pain and pleasure are often associated with one another because you can't have one without the other. Without pain, you will never know pleasure. But don't let the fear of pain keep you from experiencing the gifts of the feminine. Don't fear your sexual energy or power. Learn to embrace it and direct it in a safe and loving way. Learn to communicate your desires. Tap into that sexual energy and watch as the gateway swings open and your creative energy is unleashed.

When you are ready to sink into the blissful nature of the Divine Union, you can choose to grab your partner (or go solo!), but make sure your partner is someone you trust who respects, honors, and worships you. The Divine Union is the coming together of the Divine Masculine and Feminine (again, I'm talking energy, not gender). The masculine is the container, the structure and support that offers patience, unconditional love, vision, and penetrative energy. The masculine aims to please. The feminine is the receiver, the flow of energy itself, the healer, creation, the nurturer, and inspiration. The feminine opens through acts of devotion, and the masculine is empowered when being devoted to. This union inspires more acts of devotion, more receptivity to those acts, and finally, the reward within the cries of the Lover.

The Divine Union is sacred. It's a beautiful dance between two threads of Lovers entangled within one another. It's something to be cherished, nurtured, and explored. It's an act of honoring the divinity within our partnerships. If we believe ourselves to be goddesses and desire worship, we must honor our partners the same way. Through open communication, trust, mutual respect, and unconditional love, the Divine Union is something we can all experience, a gift from the Divine itself. The Lover opens the doors to all of the Universe's mysteries and true creative potential. Honoring this part of ourselves and being able to receive pleasure is only the beginning.

EMBODYING THE LOVER

The way of the Lover is fun, playful, and sensual. She is a muse. She is inspiration. We feel most inspired when we are in tune with our desires and seek fulfillment. And in turn, when we are tapped into that abundant flow, we find it easier to create. To embody the Lover is to embody love in all its forms. To awaken the Lover within you, open up your yoni, breathe, and open your throat. Dance, sing, find self pleasure, and seek beauty in all things. Enjoy and appreciate every part of your being. Surrender to the divine flow of energy. *Be* in the realm of the Lover. Notice the joy and ecstasy that awaits. Soak up her potent creative energy and direct it how you see fit.

If you must *do* something, fill your space with things you find beautiful. Treat yourself to a spa day. Buy yourself flowers. Dress so you feel beautiful and radiant. Embody the goddess you are. Life is meant to be experienced and enjoyed, and this is the way of the Lover: to enjoy pleasure in every moment. So often we deny ourselves pleasure, believing we must suffer or overcome some difficult feat before we can relax and enjoy ourselves. What if you sought out pleasure each and every day? What if you lived your life open to receiving all that it has in store for you? Find the sweetness and beauty in every little thing you do. And once your cup is full, give that abundance of love to others. Plan a romantic weekend getaway with your partner. Do something special for your children. Send a card to an old friend. Reach out to someone you know is having a difficult time. Smile at a stranger. Volunteer your time for a cause. Spread love for the simple fact that you have it to give. Your one act can cause a ripple effect of good deeds, inspiring others in your close circle to do the same.

SHADOW ASPECTS OF THE LOVER

We often find trouble within the Lover archetype when there isn't a mutual respect for the Divine Union, when one party receives more than they give, when someone hasn't embodied self-love before giving to others, when there is neglect or abuse of some kind, when someone is looking for love in all the wrong places, or when we project our issues onto our partners. The shadow aspects of the Lover also include obsessing over love, chasing love, or using love to manipulate others. This shadow comes through in those who are obsessed with someone or something to the point of it becoming self-destructive. As with everything in life, there needs to be a healthy balance. There is a fine line between passion and obsession. True love is unconditional.

LOVER
REFLECTION QUESTIONS

$\mathcal{O}$ What brings you joy?

$\mathcal{O}$ What gives you pleasure?

$\mathcal{O}$ Are you depriving yourself of self-love, or do you have a regular self-care routine set in place?

$\mathcal{O}$ Do you allow yourself to receive?

$\mathcal{O}$ Do you have a strong foundation of self-love?

$\mathcal{O}$ Do you allow yourself to be intimate, vulnerable, and seen by your partner? If not, what's preventing you from being vulnerable?

$\mathcal{O}$ What does your unique sexual and creative expression look like?

$\mathcal{O}$ In what ways are you called to explore the Divine Union?

GODDESSES TO WORK WITH
THAT EMBODY THE LOVER

⊘ Aphrodite:
Greek goddess of love, beauty, and fertility

⊘ Venus:
Roman goddess of love, beauty, and fertility

⊘ Ishtar:
Babylonian goddess of love, fertility, and justice

⊘ Isis:
Egyptian goddess of love, motherhood, and magic

⊘ Kuan Yin:
Chinese Bodhisattva, Goddess of mercy and
compassion

⊘ Hera:
Greek goddess of love and marriage

⊘ Juno:
Roman goddess of love and marriage

𝒪 Sophia:

Gnostic mother goddess of wisdom

𝒪 Hathor:

Egyptian goddess of women, the sky, fertility, and love

𝒪 Oshun:

African Yoruba goddess of love and fertility

𝒪 Parvati:

Hindu goddess of fertility, love, beauty, and marriage

𝒪 Rhiannon:

Welsh goddess of fertility and inspiration

LOVER
RITUAL

This ritual requires you to take a bath. If you don't have a bathtub, no worries; you can substitute a shower instead. You will be calling on the goddess Aphrodite for this ritual, but you can make substitutions as you see fit.

Materials Needed:

○ Fresh flowers

○ Fragrances or essential oils

○ Candles

○ Music[1]

Begin this ritual by drawing a bath to your preferred temperature. Take extra time to make this bath special. You aren't just taking a bath for the sake of getting clean. This bath is to honor Aphrodite and yourself as the goddess you are, to make yourself feel beautiful, loved, and worshipped, and to be reborn from the sea foam, just as Aphrodite rose out of the ocean. You are the goddess tonight.

---

1 You can find a curated playlist for the Lover Ritual at www.courtneytiffany.com/femininearchetypes

Set the mood for this ritual by turning on some soothing instrumental music, carefully lighting candles, and turning off the lights. If you can afford fresh flowers, then splurge and buy your favorite kind and put them in a vase in your bathroom. You could also buy roses and put the rose petals in the bathwater. Add essential oils to your water as well. Some of my favorites are lavender and jasmine. If you want to add a bath bomb or any other ingredients to the bath, do so. If you have rose quartz crystals, this would be a great opportunity to place them around your candles. You want to create a peaceful, spa-like space for yourself.

If you take regular baths as part of your self-care routine, I would encourage you to up the ante and do something extra special for this ritual bath. We don't want this ritual bath to be like all of the others. We want to embody Aphrodite and the Lover in this space, to connect with ourselves.

When you have your space set up, begin to disrobe, preferably in front of a mirror. Take a few extra moments here to admire your beautiful body in the mirror. Notice all the little freckles, scars, or stretch marks. Notice how each one tells a story. Each one is a part of you, making you unique and beautiful. If you're having trouble recognizing how beautiful you are, close your eyes and feel your heart swell. Focus on your heart chakra and feel it expand as you breathe. Once your heart chakra feels like it's radiating love, send that love to any areas of your body that make you feel uncomfortable. You are perfect just the way you are. You are beautiful and lovely. It's important you remind yourself of that.

When you are ready, go ahead and step into the bathtub. Sit back and relax, allowing the warm waters to lap around you. Then, send up a prayer to Aphrodite. If you are at a loss for words or are unsure of how to communicate with the goddess of love and beauty, you can say something like:

Aphrodite, goddess of love,
please help me remember my beauty and worth.
Guide me to see all the beauty around and within me.
Open my heart to receive love
and consume me with passion so I might create the things
I long for in this world.

If you want to ask her for guidance so you can remember how worthy you are of love and abundance, you can. You can make this as personal as possible. Whatever you want to say is between you and the goddess. By making your ritual personal and inviting, you will be able to establish a stronger relationship with her and open up a deeper line of communication.

While in your bath, open your heart up to Aphrodite and let her flow in and consume you with her radiance and love. Ask her to guide you in your life so you can embrace more love. Feel the emotions as they swell up within you. Let them move through you. After you establish your connection with Aphrodite and ask her to bathe you in divine love and beauty, remember to say a quick thank you for the gifts she has bestowed upon you. Stay in your bath as long as you'd like. Enjoy yourself.

When you go to drain the water out of your tub (or turn off the water in the shower), pay attention to the drain. All of the water flowing away is a representation of the self-doubt and thoughts of unworthiness, ugliness, and self-hatred. Every negative emotion you've had with lovers in the past or with yourself is now being whisked away. Aphrodite has washed away all of these thoughts and emotions.

As you step out of the ritual bathtub or shower, notice the confidence, love, and beauty you radiate. You are a goddess. You are a diamond, radiating your brilliance to the world. If you feel called to celebrate your new beautiful being, then dance naked in front of the mirror! Celebrate every curve, every line, and every spark of divinity that resides within you. Dancing allows you to embody the Divine Feminine more easily. The feminine needs to move; she needs to be able to be expressed freely. Allow yourself to sway and be seduced by your image. Rock your pelvis and open up your yoni in a way that makes you feel sensual and beautiful.

Working with the goddess of love can be very emotional sometimes. You might feel like your heart is going to burst from all of the divine love, or you might be moved to tears as painful memories are brought to the surface. Whatever comes up for you, know that it is meant to happen. Don't question it. Working with goddesses and archetypes is going to look different for everyone. The Divine only reveals what we need in any particular moment, and since we are all on different paths and journeys, we need to trust that we will be given exactly what we need in that moment. Aphrodite wants you to remember how to experience pleasure. She wants you to move in a way that embodies your beautiful female expression. You are every part beautiful and every part perfect. Feel it. Embrace it. Accept it. Love it.

THE WITCH

Just the word "witch" holds much allure and mysticism. The Witch archetype has been misunderstood for thousands of years, causing many to be burned at the stake, hung, or wrongfully imprisoned just under the suspicion of being one. Religious propaganda spread the idea of the Witch as a woman who consorts with the devil, and in books and movies, they are often portrayed as hags, evil-doers, and Satanists. But I think of the Witch as a woman who knows how to heal herself. She is in touch with nature and knows the magical and medicinal properties of herbs and plants to heal others and help them feel better.

The Witch is a medicine woman. In historical times, the women who were often labeled as witches were the healers and midwives of the village. They made tinctures and performed minor procedures. They might have been seen as outcasts, but people always sought them out for their wisdom and knowledge.

The Witch is in tune with energy and knows how to manipulate it to her advantage. She is a creatrix of sorts, and she brings forth new ideas, some that might disturb the current order of things, which is why she's so often persecuted. She goes against cultural and societal expectations. The modern-day Witch might carry a few crystals in her pocket, read tarot cards for her friends, or write spells in her book of shadows. Whether or not you personally identify with the Witch, the archetype is available to all of us. Working with the Witch can teach us to harness our power. She is someone who knows how to care for and defend herself. She is strong and empowering.

The Witch understands there is mystery within the Universe. She honors the stars, knowing the planets can give us advice. She honors nature and makes sure to include elements of earth, air, fire, and water in her craft. She decorates her altar in corre-spondence with the seasons, and she usually follows the wheel of the year. The Witch teaches us to be fearless and unafraid of the dark. Within the shadows lie great jewels. The Witch is always true to herself. She knows what she wants out of life, and when she doesn't receive it, she asks her guides or creates it herself. She knows there is always a way to find her answer. She relies on spirit guides, tarot or oracle decks, and her own intuition. She trusts that all will be revealed when it's ready to be. She manifests with confidence, knowing what she asks for will come true. Her spells are imbued with her own magic, her personal stamp.

The Witch sees the magic of everyday living in small signs from her guides, occasional symbols, or repeating numbers. Messages surround her, and she knows how to tune in. A Witch knows the importance of sisterhood. A coven is traditionally made up of thirteen women, just as there are thirteen full moons every year. She knows there is power in numbers. When we practice asserting our beliefs and standing firm in our power, we can truly be free from the judgment of others, embarrassment, or shame. When we know what is true for us on a soul level, we know where we stand with unwavering faith.

The great thing about embracing the Witch is there are so many ways to do it; there is no wrong way. The Witch teaches us to release our fears, trust our intuition, and turn our power all the way on. Some of the most common symbols of the Witch include the cauldron and the broom. The cauldron is essentially a pot or container used to mix ingredients together. The Witch knows which ingredients to add to alchemize her creation into something better. She uses her cauldron to make potions, medicines, or even a meal for her family, all while infusing her magical touch. The cauldron is a symbol of transformation. The broom is used to sweep away not only dirt and dust but negative energy. The Witch takes part in the ceremony of cleansing, ridding herself and her home of old, negative energy to make space for and welcome the new.

She is aware of the lunar cycles, understanding their significance and influence on her and knowing that every four weeks, a fresh start comes with the new moon. Just as the moon has phases, so does she. She is aware of the cyclical nature of life. The Witch understands balance and harmony. In nature, too much of anything can destroy an entire ecosystem. A flood can wipe out ecosystems, a tornado can destroy properties, and an earthquake can break apart the land. She seeks balance in all she does, honoring the elements when she casts her circle. In the same sense, we must strive to maintain balance and order in our lives. When we become stressed, our lives are no longer in homeostasis. The Witch understands how to restore that order. She has respect for all aspects of life, death, and rebirth. She knows she must break things down to create new possibilities. She can alchemize her world and emotions into something greater. The Witch understands that she is often misunderstood, for she knows things not of this world. She hears and sees things others cannot. She is the wisdom keeper, the diviner of mysteries, the conjurer of spells.

HEALING THE WITCH WOUND

The witch wound has probably existed since the first generation of accused women were persecuted in the fifteenth century, perhaps even before that. The witch wound is a deep-seated karmic fear of being persecuted for practicing witchcraft or doing things that might appear as witchcraft to others. It can paralyze you from sharing your esoteric gifts and prevent you from being curious and exploring things you are drawn to for fear of judgment.

Karmic and ancestral wounds are often buried deep within our unconscious, and it might take a spiritual awakening or dark night of the soul to uncover them. There are a lot of things in life we do for reasons we don't always understand. There are things we are drawn to or avoid without explanation, and it's often the result of those karmic belongings we brought with us when we chose to inhabit a body on Earth.

Like all trauma and wounds, though, they don't go away on their own. No matter how hard we try to suppress them, avoid them, or drown them out with drugs, food, and alcohol, they will continue to resurface and peek through until we are ready to deal with them. Ultimately, this is what living on Earth is all about: working through all our baggage to grow as a person and find peace. So when we are ready to go into our shadow self and work with the wounding, we can heal and move forward.

Those of us who carry a witch wound can feel the pull of the noose around our necks, our skin starting to blister and numb as fires are lit at the pyres, our clothes catching fire. It is a fear of gossip, words spoken behind your back, whispers entwined with your name. It is a fear of false perception. Those who aren't familiar with witches think you sold your soul to the devil and worship at his feet. The unexplored witch wound is what keeps many intuitive beings and healers hidden away behind closed doors, afraid of sharing their esoteric gifts with others.

For me, I've always been fascinated by witches—their craft, symbols, and mystery. I grew up watching *Hocus Pocus* on repeat in the autumn (something I still love to do) and reading any and every book with a witch involved. I was drawn to the magic, mysticism, and mystery. I started writing spells when I was ten years old. What started as a fun thing to do with my friends during sleepovers became a quiet practice of mine. I've spent hours researching the occult, herbalism, spellcrafting, and the history of witch persecutions, yet there was always something stopping me from actually diving in and practicing myself. I loved learning about it all, but actually practicing it was an entirely different endeavor.

I had a past-life regression once and found out I had been persecuted and hanged as a witch in a previous lifetime. The psychic who told me this also pointed out that I never wore things tightly around my neck, such as chokers or scarves. That was true, but I had never consciously thought about it until then. It wasn't until years later that I put it all together. I was dealing with a karmic witch wound. I hid my passions and "weird" interests for *years* for fear of being persecuted again on a subconscious level.

It's so important for us to recognize this trauma we carry, this fear of being hunted down and burned at the stake, because perhaps in another lifetime we were. Thankfully, we now live in the twenty-first century. There is no need to fear persecution, at least not in the modern Western world. Most of us are now free to call ourselves whatever we want. We have the freedom to call ourselves a Witch and not be punished for it. It's time to own our gifts as intuitive beings, psychics, healers, herbalists, midwives, sensitives, empaths, Crones, tarot readers, or reiki practitioners and share them with the world.

It's time to release the fear and embrace our gifts. It's time to reclaim the word so we can reclaim our power and sovereignty. No longer do we have to live in fear. When we heal the witch wound within us, we are healing the centuries of oppression we've been carrying. We are able to live our lives in an authentic manner. Healing the witch wound allows us to stand firm in our power and beliefs. It allows us to have autonomy and freely make our own decisions without being swayed by others. When we choose to consciously look at this wounding deep within us and get real about what is preventing us from sharing our gifts, we are able to transmute the fear into empowered action.

I believe it's our duty, right here and now, to heal ourselves from all the karmic, ancestral, and generational wounds we carry. By doing so, not only will we create a better future for the next generations, but we'll heal Mother Earth. Healing the witch wound is just one aspect of this, but it could very well be the Witch archetype that leads us back into harmony.

EMBODYING THE WITCH

Embodying the Witch requires us to honor our true nature and harness our power. Learn to trust your intuition, and don't shy away from your magic. The Witch archetype can help us all reclaim our fierce feminine gifts. She helps us open up to the mysteries. One of my favorite quotes is from Roald Dahl, who said, "Those who don't believe in magic will never find it." I couldn't agree more with this sentiment. If you don't believe in your power, your magic, you'll never see it and you'll never be able to tap into it and harness it. If you don't believe magic exists, then it doesn't. But if you believe you are strong, powerful, and have the ability to create any life you want, then you will do so.

To access your inner Witch is to access your inner power and reclaim all the parts of yourself that you keep hidden from others. The Witch has her own mysterious way of being, one that we might never fully understand with our human ways of thinking, but she offers us a portal. Your esoteric gifts are meant to be used, shared, and honored. Whether you speak to your spirit guides, offer healing services, or create natural remedies, those are all beautiful gifts. Those aren't things to be ashamed of. A lot of women try to hide their magic, afraid of what others will think of them because it's not the norm. Well, what if it could be? What if more women reclaimed their inner Witch and made those esoteric gifts the norm? What if there was a Witch revolution? Right now, in this moment, we are creating a new reality. We are realizing the damage that has been done to our Earth, and we are implementing new ways of living and doing business that will produce significantly less damage to the world: investing in renewable resources, not giving in to fast fashion or single-use plastics, and being more environmentally conscious. I believe this way of life is due in part to the Witch. Whether that is the label you want to place on it or not makes no difference. It's the Witch that honors the natural cycles of the land. The Witches that have been burned and ridiculed will be the ones who pave a way forward for all of us.

Most modern Witches are activists. When you identify as a Witch, you are well aware of the oppression that's been present for centuries. Witches will always take the side of the oppressed, seeking justice for those wrongly accused. Whether calling for protection of the environment, civil rights, or animal welfare, every Witch fights for those who can't speak for themselves.

SHADOW ASPECTS OF THE WITCH

With that being said, I should also mention the shadow aspects of the Witch. These come forth when a Witch is constantly causing harm to others with hexes and curses. As mentioned, a Witch lives close to the land and understands how to transform energy. But if someone is constantly in a place of negativity, placing blame and trying to protect their ego, they are not living in the highest expression of the Witch. A Witch is here to break the rules, help make a change, and advocate for the oppressed, but that shouldn't include tearing others down. The Witch shouldn't try to gain power over others, for that is not the most divinely expressed version of this archetype.

WITCH
REFLECTION QUESTIONS

O What feelings arise for you when you think of the thousands of innocent lives that were taken for being labeled a "witch"?

O What are your feelings about the word "witch"?

O In what moments in life did you have to rely on yourself and your intuition to heal?

O What natural gifts do you have that might seem weird to others?

O Would you consider yourself a healer?

O How can you live closer to the land? How can you honor the ways of Mother Nature?

O What are some ways you can reclaim your power?

GODDESSES TO WORK WITH
THAT EMBODY THE WITCH

O Hekate:
Greek goddess of the crossroads, the night, the moon, witchcraft, and magick; Queen of Witches

O Freyja:
Norse goddess of love, fertility, and magick (specifically seidr)

O Morrigan:
Celtic goddess of battle, death, and prophecy

O Morgan Le Fay:
Welsh enchantress, Queen of Fairies, Priestess of Avalon

O Cerridwen:
Celtic goddess of inspiration and rebirth, keeper of the cauldron

WITCH
RITUAL

Witchcraft is based on ritual. With any spell you cast or potion you brew, there is often a set of steps you must take before you can proceed. Ritual is always important, as it helps us hold a greater meaning to what we are performing. You might think you're just creating a delicious meal for your family, but a kitchen Witch might be stirring in ingredients that bring love and prosperity. You might send a simple prayer to a guardian angel, ancestor, or God for the protection of you or a loved one, but the Witch invokes the powers of the goddess to carry her through. For this ritual, you will be casting your own spell of sorts, invoking a goddess, and reclaiming your power.

Materials Needed:

- A candle to represent the fire element

- A cup of water to represent the water element

- Salt or a local plant to represent the earth element

- A feather to represent the air element

Place your earth element (salt or plant) to the north, your water element (cup) to the west, your fire element (candle) to the south, and your air element (feather) to the east. Feel free to find other substitutions for the elements, but the direction in which they are placed should remain the same. If you don't have a feather on hand, try this fun trick. Ask the Universe to send one your way and see how long it takes to find you.

Place each object around you and cast your circle by walking in a clockwise direction. As you place each item, start with the north and say, "I ask the element of earth to bless this circle," then place your object on the ground. Repeat for the next three elements as you cast your circle ("I ask the element of water to bless this circle," and so on). Once you are done, have a seat within your circle.

Close your eyes and picture yourself walking outside barefoot in the moonlight. Notice your surroundings in your meditation. Start taking slow, deep breaths all the way to your womb space. Place your hands on your womb or sacral chakra if this helps you focus your energy. This is where the mysteries lie. When you are ready, ask the goddess to reveal herself to you. You can call on any goddess of your choosing, or you can even call on Mother Earth. If you are not ready and open to meet her, she isn't going to waste her time showing up, so you must really focus on her energy and want her to share her wisdom with you. Breathe in her energy and feel her fill up your body with her magic. Feel her power pulse through your veins and into your fingertips. Some will see the goddess herself; others will feel or hear her. No matter how she shows up for you, know that it is perfect.

Ask the goddess to remind you of your power. Imagine a line of source energy penetrating into your power. This could be coming up from the ground and entering your womb space, or it could be a connection between you and the goddess, a direct source of power permeating into your solar plexus. Breathe it in and let it fill you up. Soak in all of the magic as you let it pulsate through your body. Your body knows. Your feminine nature knows. You know how strong you are; sometimes you just need a little reminder. Picture your power, strength, and magic flowing to and through you. What color is it? What does it look like? How does it move? Pay attention to the little details. Sit here in your circle as long as you'd like. Surrender to the mysteries of the Divine. Reclaim your esoteric gifts, your inner Witch, and your power. Unleash your magic and wield it to your advantage. Let it work for you to guide you in life. Stay here in this energy as long as you'd like. You can even turn on some music and sink into the space where the mysteries are held.

When you are done with your meditation, thank the goddess for everything she bestowed upon you. Watch her as she retreats back into the darkness from which she came. Bring your breath back into your body. Wiggle your toes and fingers before you open your eyes, bringing your awareness back to where you are sitting. Close your circle by gathering each element one at a time counter-clockwise, thanking each element as you go along.

This is a ritual you can do time and time again. You can do this for however long you'd like. Perhaps you'll start off small with just five or ten minutes and work your way up to an hour. The deeper you are willing to go here, the more will be revealed to you. With all magic, however much you put in is how much you will receive.

THE MOTHER

This is the archetype that unites us all: the Mother, the one from which we are all born. Our life on this planet begins within the womb of the Mother. She is the one who nurtures and cares for us. The first relationships we have in this world are the ones created with our mothers. It's our first understanding of connection, trust, and commitment. Our survival depends on our mothers during our days of infancy. They provide us with the life-sustaining milk that will help us grow. As any mother will tell you, the bond between mother and child is like no other. The archetype of the Mother is one of nurturing and unconditional love. She embodies fertility, nourishment, and patience. She encourages her children to grow into self-sufficient adults, pouring all her love and warmth into them. As mothers, we encourage our children to grow, learn, and evolve. We hope that if we do our jobs right, one day they will fly out of the nest on their own.

Whether you are an actual mother or not does not matter. To embody this archetype, you must simply invest your time and energy into something other than yourself and wish for it to be successful, whether that is a project, a book, music, a pet, or a plant. As women, we have the amazing ability to create and sustain life. It starts deep within our wombs. When we sink into this part of our bodies, we are able to access great wisdom and ancient feminine understanding. This is the residing place of Shakti, the creative life force energy. We are able to tap into and unleash this energy to create new life. Again, I'm not just talking about babies. You can create a new business, a passion project, or a piece of artwork. Whatever you want to bring into existence, it starts with tapping into the creative life force within you.

As mentioned earlier, the step before becoming the Mother within the triple goddess is the Maiden. She is the one who gathers and prepares for creation. Motherhood is the act of that creation, bringing that very thing into being. As mothers, we bring this life out into the world, and we nurture it, feed it, and watch it grow. We know we are successful when we can release our grasp and watch our creation take off without us.

This can look like a child moving out on their own for the first time, or it could mean taking a step back from your creation and letting someone else manage it. When we release our grip, we then step into the Crone archetype and are able to view our lives from a different perspective.

For many of us, we spend a lot of time embodying the Mother archetype. If you've ever had to care for another person, whether it was an elderly member of the family, babysitting, or even holding your friend's hair out of their face when they were sick, you, my friend, have embodied the Mother. The Mother comes with a sense of love, nourishment, and knowledge of how to care for another person. Seeing others' needs met brings satisfaction to this archetype. In its most divine expression, it's a very selfless archetype, for it puts other people's needs before its own. To embody the Mother is to nurture something into existence and care for it. It's fascinating to see young children do this with dolls while playing mother or babysitter. It's a deeply embedded archetype that is responsible for all of existence.

The Mother is there to help us, encourage us, and give us the guidance we need so we may find our way on our own. We lean on her for support in times of need or stress. Even if you don't have a mother figure in your life, you can call on Mother Earth and sink into earth energy at any time, but especially if you feel flighty or confused. To me, earth energy is Mother energy, and we can work with nature to help us feel grounded and stabilized. She helps us clear the fog of our lives and steers us in the right direction.

HEALING THE MOTHER WOUND

Like the Witch, there is also a wound around the Mother archetype. Embodying this archetype can bring up a lot of wounds or trauma surrounding our own mothers. Some people don't have loving, nurturing mothers; instead, they have had to mother themselves. Mothers who haven't healed themselves might take their burdens out on their children. They can be critical, disapproving, unloving, manipulative, passive-aggressive, or abusive. It's important to distance yourself, whether emotionally or physically, if this is the case so you may focus on your healing around the Mother archetype. Mothers, who we might somewhat idolize in our subconscious, are also human and make mistakes. If I've learned anything from becoming a mother myself, it is that there is no manual, and you learn alongside your children.

Sometimes we have to lean into Mother archetypes like Demeter or Mama Gaia to feel held and supported. We have to learn to forgive and release all of the wounding our mothers might have inflicted on us. It's so easy for us to blame our mothers for things, whether it's not living up to our expectations of what a mother should be or being absent or abusive. To truly heal the mother wound, we must learn to forgive. We must recognize that our mothers are individuals. They are simply human beings who were trying to do their best. We are all prone to making mistakes; none of us are perfect. When we can move past that and take responsibility for our actions, rather than place blame on the lack of positive attention our mother gave us, we can heal and be free.

This can be extremely emotional, as this wound runs deep. Healing doesn't occur overnight. Many people prefer to bury their emotions and not address them, but if we are to live a life of authenticity, we must come to terms with our shadows and wounds. We must learn to heal and work through our emotions and forgive those who may not have given us their all. Leaning into the Mother archetype and the appropriate goddesses can help us in our search for support and guidance, and it can be quite comforting and healing. Talking to other women we perceive as mothers can also help with this. If you have a mother figure in your life or an older woman you can go to for advice or support, lean on them. The mother(s) we were given in this lifetime can teach us lessons for our personal growth and evolution.

Some women are lucky to call their mothers their best friends, and some don't have a relationship with her at all. It's important, when uncovering the Mother archetype, to look at your relationship with your mother or mother figure. What kind of relationship do you have with her? If there is pain there, are you able to forgive her for not showing up how you needed her to?

When a lot of wounding shows up around the Mother archetype, it's important to turn to your inner child. Sometimes you have to nurture that part of yourself and show up as the mother you did not have, giving yourself the comfort you wished you had received. You have to show up as your own cheerleader. Being your own mother might include taking care of your body and mental health. How do you treat yourself on a daily basis? Do you practice self-compassion? I often find myself turning to the earth energy of Mama Gaia to help me ground and receive comfort. Taking a walk in the grass barefoot, going for a hike, or tending to my garden all help me stay connected to the great Mother. If you can heal the mother wound within yourself, you can break the generational cycle of wounding and bring love and nourishment to those who will come after you.

Regardless of mother wounds, the Mother is an archetype that's accessible to each and every one of us, and it can provide great healing and clarity in our lives, helping us nurture our passion projects and spread love to others.

EMBODYING THE MOTHER

To embody the Mother, you must take care of and nurture others. It requires being a beacon of hope and a stable source of comfort, giving unconditional love to another. To embody the Mother within requires you to heal your inner child. Be all of these things for others as well as yourself. The Mother can intuitively understand what someone needs at a glance. She holds emotional and energetic space for others, providing whatever substance they need. The Mother receives fulfillment in watching her children, friend, pet, or project grow, transform, and evolve under her watchful eye. She is working to heal her wounds around the Mother archetype, and ideally will take it a step further to heal any generational mother wounds in her maternal lineage as well.

SHADOW ASPECTS OF THE MOTHER

The shadow aspect of the Mother archetype is seen in a woman who is emotionally or physically abusive or acts in destructive ways toward her child. The Mother's natural progression is that of the Crone. Eventually, the time will come when all her birds must leave the nest. Hindering a child's growth by refusing to let them leave or smothering them can prove to be harmful to the child.

Shadow aspects of the Mother can also be displayed in relationships where you constantly find yourself seeking approval. Unconsciously going above and beyond and searching for validation might be indicative of the need for inner child healing. Women in a matriarchal or maternal role, such as a teacher or guide, should not misuse their position to manipulate or domineer others.

MOTHER
REFLECTION QUESTIONS

○ What is your relationship with your mother like?

○ In what ways do you (or do you need to) mother your-self? Do you practice self-compassion, or are you hard on yourself? Why do you think that is?

○ If you have children, what is your relationship with them like? Do you wish it were different in any way?

○ Are you holding on to any mother wounds? If so, what are they?

○ How else do you embody the Mother in your life? Do you take care of pets, plants, elders, etc.?

○ Take a moment to tune into your inner child. Is there anything she needs?

GODDESSES TO WORK WITH
THAT EMBODY THE MOTHER

○ Gaia:

  Greek goddess of the Earth

○ Demeter:

  Greek goddess of the harvest

○ Frigg:

  Norse goddess of marriage and fertility

○ Danu:

  Celtic mother goddess

○ Isis:

  Egyptian goddess of love, motherhood, and magic

○ Brigid:

  Celtic goddess of healers, poets, smiths, and childbirth

○ Parvati:

  Hindu goddess of fertility, love, beauty, and marriage

MOTHER
RITUAL

———————

Mother energy naturally pulsates through the Earth, and if you can go outside for this ritual, that would be best. The full moon is a time for releasing and letting go, which is the perfect accompaniment to shedding your old skin and being reborn. Release the things that are hindering you from flying on your own. Let go of the strings holding you down. Cut the cords that have you stuck in old patterns and beliefs. Let the Mother nurture you while you grow into the amazing person you were born to be. Let her remove any stress, worries, or obstacles so you may spread your wings freely.

Materials Needed:

- 1 or 2 blankets

During a full moon (when the moon is in her Mother phase), go outside, lay your blanket on the ground (the closer to the Earth the better), and look up at the night sky. Take a moment to listen to the natural world around you. Do you hear crickets or birds? Can you see the stars, or is it cloudy? If you have a heavy blanket, place this one on top of you. When you are ready to begin, close your eyes and let your mind go blank. Focus on the weight of the heavy blanket on top of you and feel yourself slowly sink into the depths of the Earth.

Imagine Mother Earth slowly rocking you in her arms as she carries you down into her depths underground, into the womb of the Earth. She is your mother, and you are her babe. Curl up into a ball and let her hold you here. Pay attention to any thoughts or feelings that arise. Sink further into her loving embrace and picture a cord travelling from your belly button into the walls of her womb, connecting you to her. Once you establish a connection, breathe in the nourishment she wishes to give you. Feel as her energy pulsates through the umbilical cord into your body. Notice the love, care, and nourishment she grants you. Ask her for anything else you might need. Strength, courage, hope, and peace are all up for the taking. The Mother will grant you everything you desire. Ask and ye shall receive. You may also ask her to take any burdens off your shoulders, whether it be pain, fear, doubt, or unworthiness. She wants to sustain you and empower you before you return above ground. You are in a cocoon, growing your wings and gaining your strength before you will be reborn. Sit in her womb for as long as you need to.

When you are ready to be reborn, slowly detach yourself from her walls and picture the umbilical cord breaking from your abdomen and slowly retreating back into the Earth. You are now radiating with the love and wisdom of the Mother. You are ready to take on a new adventure, like a butterfly learning to fly for the first time.

As you make your way back up to the Earth's surface, you must push and crawl your way out. You must learn to do this part on your own. The Earth crumbles easily in your hands. She gives way to you, and you continue to push your way toward the surface. A butterfly must stretch and spread her wings before she can fly. You, too, must prove you can do this on your own. Your hand breaks above the surface, and the fresh night air fills your lungs. Bring your attention back to your body, your hands, your arms, and your chest as it rises and falls. Shed the blanket that is on top of you and slowly make your way to a standing position. Bask in the rebirth process, stand proud, and feel your body pulsate with love.

Congratulations on your rebirth. It's time to spread your wings and fly.

THE QUEEN

The Queen is an archetype of power and sovereignty. She is not reserved for those born with royal blood but is for all women in charge of their personal kingdoms. The Queen is someone who doesn't play by the rules, for she is the one who makes the rules. She has her own rulebook and knows what works. She is sovereign. A Queen is conscious of how her actions and decisions will impact those in her kingdom. She is constantly thinking of others when it is her time to lead. She is strong and independent, and she believes in her intuition. She is so connected to herself that she knows what she needs and how to manifest it. She has an innate inner power that can't be messed with.

A Queen is fearless because she has already faced her inner demons. She has overcome many obstacles and has sat with her shadows and accepted them for what they are and the lessons they have taught her. She understands that we all have light and dark parts of ourselves; we are all capable of good and evil. This is precisely how she comes out on top. She has been to hell and back and continuously picks herself back up. She laughs in the face of danger because she has run with the wolves herself. She is a phoenix who has risen from the ashes. She is constantly growing and evolving, and now she stands at the top.

To become a Queen, you can't just walk up and claim the throne; you have to earn it. A Queen has built her throne through blood, sweat, and tears. She is the boss, the executive. She has worked hard to be where she is and has faced many difficulties. Things typically aren't just handed to her; she has had to endure change and growing pains. It is because of this that she knows her true value. She knows she is worthy of everything she has received.

The Queen is a woman who no longer silences her voice and stands on the sidelines of her life. She knows how to speak her mind. She knows that everyone is entitled to their opinions and doesn't get upset when someone shares theirs, even if she might not agree with them. She knows her inner truth. A Queen is sovereign and knows that letting others make her decisions would be a detriment to her.

To be sovereign, you must be above another's rule, but we can take this a step further and say you must also not be swayed by their opinions. In today's world, people love to share their opinions about what you *should* do, but ultimately, what matters is if the decisions you make are in alignment with your highest and greatest good. Do you feel confident in your decisions, or are you trying to please others, going against your better judgment? To really step into this archetype, you must learn to make decisions based on your beliefs from a soul-centered place. You must accept that you can't please everyone.

Everyone on this planet has a different set of beliefs. We must learn to accept that instead of trying to change it. It is not our job to change the opinions of others; that is the individual's job. Beliefs are hardwired in our brains, so it takes us a long time and a lot of exposure and conditioning to change the way we think. When we are forced to make decisions, we must understand that not everyone is going to agree with us, and that's OK! Trying to please people might seem like a good idea, but the longer you continue to put others' needs before your own, the more likely you'll disappoint yourself in the end.

A Queen also knows how to set boundaries. She doesn't let others walk all over her. She no longer lets people take advantage of her good will and kindness. She likes to help others and gives when she can. She is caring and generous, but she also knows her limits. A Queen knows how to rule with grace and compassion. She is diplomatic, looking at all sides of a situation before making a decision.

EMBODYING THE QUEEN

When we embody the archetype of the Queen in our lives, we have the ability to create the kingdom we see fit. We recognize that our decisions make an impact, and we can use that information to influence how we live our lives. A Queen must take action. She isn't going to let others make decisions for her. Sure, someone can offer counsel or guidance, but the final decision always comes from her heart and mind.

To embody the Queen archetype, you must retain your power and remain sovereign in all aspects, physically, emotionally, and mentally. It's so easy to unconsciously give away your power, so I think it's important to look at some examples of how we unknowingly do so. Altering your beliefs to appease someone else gives away your power. Allowing others to manipulate you, either through flattery or power of suggestion, does not allow you to maintain your sovereignty. Holding on to things, such as relationships or careers, because they provide your ego with acceptance or validation but are otherwise toxic is detrimental. Recognize when you are taking on someone's problems as your own. Women are natural caregivers who want to fix problems, but be sure you aren't taking on those problems as your own. When you do this, when you make someone's problem your own, you are giving away your power. You can still help others and maintain your sovereignty. As a Queen, you have free will and the power to choose how and where you spend your time.

You must not fall victim or prey to manipulation or ego-boosting causes. Remember, when we discuss these archetypes, we are talking about them from a soul-aligned place, from the view of the Divine Feminine. To truly align with this archetype, you must lead from the soul, not the ego. There must be a level of soul fulfillment so you can easily make decisions you can trust. The Queen invokes in us a level of confidence because we are whole, complete, and beautiful, and we don't need others to validate that for us. The Queen takes charge of her life; she understands her power to choose and create the life she wants, and she retains her power in the process. She knows her worth and is not afraid to ask for what she wants. She knows she deserves the life she's always wanted. She is responsible, reliable, and bold. The Queen values honesty. She is fearless in her pursuits.

SHADOW ASPECTS OF THE QUEEN

The shadow side of the Queen comes through in those who rule for power. They can be manipulative or controlling, looking to gain power over others or slipping into aggressive or destructive behaviors. It's always important to connect with your why. Why are you making your decisions? What is the underlying motivation behind what you choose to do? Are you leading from a heart-centered place or an ego-driven, fear-based place?

Answering these questions can help you align with the divine aspects of the Queen so you can truly feel empowered and ready to embrace your throne.

QUEEN
REFLECTION QUESTIONS

---

0 How do you embody the Queen throughout your day?

0 In what ways are you giving away your power?

0 Are you leading your life from an ego- or soul-driven place?

0 What makes you feel confident?

0 What boundaries have you set in place so that others don't cross them?

GODDESSES TO WORK WITH
THAT EMBODY THE QUEEN

O Persephone (after her abduction):
Greek Queen of the Underworld

O Frigg:
Norse Queen of Asgard

O Morgan Le Fay:
Welsh enchantress, Queen of Fairies, Priestess
of Avalon

O Lakshmi:
Hindu goddess of wealth, luxury, beauty, and power

O Inanna:
Sumerian love and fertility goddess, Queen of Heaven

QUEEN
RITUAL

Materials Needed:

○ Candles

○ Fruit (strawberries, pomegranate seeds, raspberries)

○ Craft supplies to make a crown

To feel like a Queen on your throne, you are going to need a crown, my dear. Whether you want to make your crown out of flowers, crystals, paper, or ribbon, make a crown you will feel happy to wear. Make a crown that truly represents the type of Queen you will be. If you see yourself ruling with authority, make the points a little taller and sharper. If you see yourself as a soft and delicate Queen, make your crown out of flowers. I've seen crowns made out of a headband, hot glue, and glitter, and I've seen ones made out of just paper and tape. This can be as easy, elaborate, or decorative as you want.

If you just absolutely don't want to make a crown and you prefer drawing, painting, or sculpting, then make your crown that way! Paint a crown on canvas or draw one on paper. Adorn it with jewels, glitter, and colors however you see fit, then hang it up somewhere you can be reminded of it every single day. Stick it on your fridge or frame it and put it in your bedroom. Don't ever lose sight of your sovereign reign. You make the rules in your life. You are responsible for your kingdom and castle. You no longer need to sit on the sidelines of your life, picking the flowers and watching life pass you by. You are in control, you decide what happens, and you get to decide what kind of life you want to have. You are a Queen.

Make this ritual an event. Light some candles, pour your favorite beverage, snack on some pomegranate seeds or strawberries. Turn it into a ceremony. This is your coronation. It's your time to step onto your throne and announce yourself as Queen.

THE PRIESTESS

The Priestess is an archetype that women have been connecting with since the dawn of time. It was women who
were once the oracles at Delphi. Priestesses kept the flame lit
in Vesta's temples, and nuns kept Brigid's sacred fire aglow.
She's the archetype of spiritual connection, ceremony, and divine guidance. She is that thread within us that causes us to
seek answers outside of ourselves. The Priestess enjoys prayer,
stillness, and meditation. She knows there are forces outside of
her guiding her way, and she understands there is more to this
life than what we can simply see. There is a greater underlying
connection. There is a reason and importance for ceremony, as
it allows us to open the doors to the great beyond and step into
a realm unseen.

The Priestess's focus is turned inward. She lives from a place of soul-based truth and alignment. She is the embodiment of the Divine Feminine. She trusts her inner knowing, is in tune with her intuition, and places it on speed dial whenever she needs to make a decision. The Priestess is devoted, honest, and faithful and lives a balanced life. She knows her purpose and trusts the Divine to lead the way. She is a servant of the gods/goddesses/ higher powers. Her life is one of servitude to the greater calling. She is deeply spiritual and may even be called to lead others toward the divine light.

To be a Priestess simply means to embody the Divine. And if you are at a place where you have come to realize that you are a part of the Divine and the Divine is a part of you, then you are a modern-day Priestess. You are able to tune out the noise in your life and turn inward, connecting with your higher self and trusting whatever comes up during that time.

The Priestess's roles have changed over the years. No longer is she committed to a life of celibacy and devotion. She doesn't need to live in the temples, apart from her community, helping only those who seek her out. There is a modern-day Priestess emerging: the woman who juggles both the spiritual world and her physical reality. She has one foot exploring the higher realms within herself and the other planted firmly on the ground. The Priestess is a woman connected to her intuition, seeking spiritual guidance and helping others remember their divinity. She is a reminder that we are all divine and we all have the ability to access our higher selves. She leads by example, offering guidance when she feels called to.

The modern-day Priestess is a revolutionary. As more people are leaving the constraints of patriarchal organized religion, she is the bridge that guides them to spiritual enlightenment. She creates a pathway for others to follow, for she has devoted her life to the Divine. She holds sacred knowledge within her, and as such, she is an active member of her community, providing a temple of refuge for others to come and seek spiritual attunement on their unique journeys toward reconnecting with their inner divinity.

Every being on this planet is able to access the Priestess archetype within them. It is a spiritual-based place we can incorporate into our daily lives. To be a Priestess, you must embody the Divine. The modern Priestess has found a way to incorporate her spiritual life into her daily living. I, for one, am a huge fan and advocate of having a daily spiritual practice. As I talked about extensively in my book *Journey to Soul*, this was something I started doing after I realized I wasn't taking enough time for myself. I started each morning with five to ten minutes of alone time (because I had two young babies who couldn't go longer than that without seeing or hearing me), and I would sit in meditation. My daily practice today changes depending on what I feel called to do. Sometimes I sit in silence, then journal.

I might pull an oracle card or two or do an entire tarot spread. I might listen to a guided meditation, perform kundalini yoga, or write in my gratitude journal. Whatever I feel called to do, whatever I think I need the most that day, I will do. But I always try to sit at my meditation pillow around the same time every day. Sometimes I only have five minutes to drop in; other times, I might have an hour. Regardless, I try to be consistent and show up every day, as this is what builds a habit. This provides time and space to reconnect to the Divine and my higher self.

Through repetitive steps, we are able to develop new habits, so if you are interested in incorporating more spiritual practices into your life, I suggest you pick the same time every day, perhaps starting with just five minutes, and sit quietly, turning your focus inward. You can start by focusing on your breathing or doing a mental body scan, focusing on areas of tension and stress and trying to bring your breath to those areas to relax them.

Connecting with the Priestess within requires you to be in touch with your intuition and higher self and to understand that everything that occurs is meant to take place and all will be revealed when it's meant to. You must learn to surrender to the unknown and have faith that everything will work out. A task that is oftentimes easier said than done, this requires you to relinquish all thoughts of control. In the stillness, we are able to connect with this part of ourselves. The Priestess is open to receiving messages. She has learned not to question what comes up, knowing and trusting that she is being shown only what can help her take the next step forward. She trusts in divine timing. She surrenders to the unknown.

Being a Priestess means living as your truest self, being in touch with who you are as a person, and letting your soul lead the way. There is no façade when it comes to the Priestess; what you see is what you get. She makes decisions from a place of immense wisdom and understanding. She is in complete balance and pure alignment of mind, body, and soul. The modern Priestess doesn't need to abandon her life and live in solitude; she doesn't need to shut the world out. She has found a way to blend her life with her spirituality. She dances along the line of the physical and spiritual. She has arranged it so she only has time for what brings her joy and happiness. She has let go of drama, gossip, and negative people, and she has created a life truly worth living in her eyes. She embodies love and acceptance in everything she does. She allows us to heal so we may, in turn, help others do the same.

The Priestess is the midwife of the spiritual journey. She ushers forth those seeking more answers. She facilitates the journey inward. She shows others how to live a more balanced and soul-aligned life by being an example for them. Above all, the Priestess pushes us to know the truth of ourselves, others, and the world. She is the embodiment of feminine wisdom, pushing us to know our truth and reclaim our intuition as power and divine wisdom. She treats her life as a sacred act, a way of being so in tune with her heart, in sync with her path forward, and unafraid of her shadows that she is unshakable.

EMBODYING THE PRIESTESS

To embody the Priestess is to embrace a soul-led life and have trust and faith in the Divine/Universe/God. She keeps her eyes open for signs and knows she holds within her all the wisdom and guidance she needs. To be a Priestess is to live by example. It's not about going out and preaching, telling others how to live; it's about showing them. A Priestess has confidence and the ability to surrender to the unknown. She embraces all the wisdom life has to offer, maintaining a beautiful symbiotic relationship with the Divine.

What a Priestess actually looks like and does will vary from person to person. She might choose to use her platform in devotion to a goddess or simply to light a candle each day. She might teach, write, or create something in honor of the Divine. She can broadcast it or keep it to herself. But regardless of what she does, she continues to show up and devote time to her spiritual expansion.

SHADOW ASPECTS OF THE PRIESTESS

Be wary of the shadow aspect of the Priestess. This tends to manifest when the woman channeling divine messages doesn't implement what she's teaching into her own life. She guides others to live a certain way but neglects to implement the same tools in her practice. The Priestess leads by example. She can't say one thing and then do another; that doesn't make it her truth.

PRIESTESS
REFLECTION QUESTIONS

O Are you currently living in a way that is in sync with your truth and values? If not, what needs to change?

O How can you deepen your connection with the Divine?

O In what ways do you embody the Priestess?

O How do you choose to honor the Divine?

O Do you currently have a routine spiritual practice? If not, how can you implement five to ten minutes into your day to reconnect with your soul self?

GODDESSES TO WORK WITH
THAT EMBODY THE PRIESTESS

O Hestia:

Greek goddess of hearth and home, Keeper of the Eternal Flame

O Vesta:

Roman goddess of hearth and home, Keeper of the Eternal Flame

O Morgan Le Fay:

Welsh enchantress, Queen of Fairies, Priestess of Avalon

O Isis:

Egyptian goddess of love, motherhood, and magic

PRIESTESS
RITUAL

———————

Materials Needed:

O Pen and paper

For this ritual, you will be making a craft. I find it helpful to have an art piece or memento to put on my altar or adorn my home with that reminds me of my experience with a goddess. Additionally, making a craft allows me to tap into my creative energy and let the Divine Feminine flow through me.

In this ritual, you will be making a mandala. The word *mandala* is Sanskrit for "circle," hence why it is made up of multiple layers of circles. If you are unfamiliar with a mandala, an internet search will bring up several examples.

Start with a simple circle and build out from there, adding each layer one at a time. Making a mandala can put us in a trance-like state. You can get lost in what you are doing, much like when you meditate. I recommend you set aside some uninterrupted quiet time to complete this. Don't worry about it being perfect; that is not what this is about. The purpose is to help you connect with your center point, enlighten your mind, and perhaps encourage healing. As each layer is added, think of it as representing a piece of wisdom the Priestess archetype has shared with you, a piece of your inner bud unfolding and blossoming.

The Priestess keeps her focus inward on her soul, and the mandala is a useful tool to help us facilitate that. If you want to print out a mandala and trace it to practice first, you can, but try your best not to think too hard about it. It's important to get into the habit of leaving your inner critic at the door. Don't worry if things aren't symmetrical. It's uniquely yours. This is for your eyes only.

Imagine yourself in the center of the mandala and watch as it expands and grows, just as we all do. We all start off this life as a tiny egg, only to get bigger, stronger, and wiser with each passing day. Allow this ritual to connect you with the infinite wisdom of the Universe. You may find this activity to be extremely relaxing; it could even help with some anxiety you might be experiencing. You might find you like the process of creating mandalas and add it to your list of hobbies.

If you want to do something a little extra, I invite you to add color to the layers of your mandala or paint a canvas first, then add the mandala on top of it. Whatever you choose to do, may the Priestess's wisdom and spiritual guidance radiate through you.

THE HEARTH KEEPER

The Hearth Keeper might not seem like your typical archetype, but once upon a time, the hearth was the central point of the home. It provided warmth and allowed its patrons to cook their food. It was a place where everyone gathered and as such, it was lit most of the day. When it was not in use, its coals were allowed to smolder so a fire could be made at a moment's notice. There was an art to keeping the flame of the house aglow. It took constant attention and specific knowledge about what woods and kindling burned best and longest. There are two aspects of the Hearth Keeper to discuss, the home life and spiritual life.

In her home life, the Hearth Keeper is in touch with her domestic duties. She finds purpose and peace in keeping her household in order. While it might seem simplistic, the Hearth Keeper tidies, cleans, and organizes the household for optimal performance. As the domestic goddess, the Hearth Keeper recognizes that there is something extremely therapeutic in washing away the dirt and grime and making the home sparkle again. She can get lost in her chores, allowing her mind to quiet and letting the peace of her surroundings swallow her. It gives her time to turn inward.

The Hearth Keeper, Keeper of the Flame, Hearth Witch, or whatever label you choose for her resembles the domestic goddess. She is the homemaker, housewife, or stay-at-home mom we know of today. She loves making things from scratch. She is a cook, seamstress, handywoman, or gardener. She can be all of the above or none of them. She is in tune with the energy of her home and seeks to maintain its balance. She uses her broom to push out the dirt, dust, and negative energy and only invites the good in. She knows home is where the heart is, and her home is inviting, warm, and full of love. She keeps her household in balance. She tends to the flames of all of those around her. You might consider her a caregiver of sorts, always taking stock of what goes on around her and what needs mending.

In the spiritual life of the Hearth Keeper, fire is the primary symbol, as it represents the eternal spirit that resides not only in the hearth but in each one of us. This spirit is our inner flame, a representation of our soul. Our inner light only goes out when our soul departs from this world and into the next. The Hearth Keeper recognizes the inner flame within each individual. It burns brightly when we are passionate and deeply consumed by something we find value in. We follow the flame throughout our lifetimes and feed it by doing the things we love. We fuel its flame when we find work that gives us purpose and meaning. It engulfs us when we fall in love. The inner flame is our spirit, driving us in any given moment. It's our connection to Source, our reminder that its embers will forever burn as long as we have breath in our lungs.

The Hearth Keeper pays mind to those who live under her roof. She is sometimes the keeper of other flames as well. She might be a mother, breastfeeding her child, giving her newborn baby life and sustenance, and fueling that little flame to grow bigger and stronger each day. The Hearth Keeper might have older flames to tend to as a caretaker of someone she loves. She ensures their flame is kept lit as best she can, tending the fire and breathing oxygen into it. The Hearth Keeper is aware of her surroundings and the people at her hearth. She is determined to make sure everyone she lives with is on their right path. She is a mentor and a guide in this capacity. She carries the torch to light the way for others.

In yoga class, instructors usually end their class by saying, "The light in me honors the light within you. Namaste." There is a light within all of us. It represents our soul being. It's important we honor that part of ourselves. Sometimes, though, those lights can be dimmed when we play small, dumb ourselves down, decide not to speak up, or become depressed. The Western world is so inundated with the idea of keeping our lights dim because by doing so, we blend in. We fear shining our light out of judgment, afraid of what others will say if we put ourselves in the spotlight. Or perhaps we don't want to draw attention to ourselves or outshine others.

The Hearth Keeper is a necessary archetype to explore when we are in the midst of major healing and shadow work. She is the Keeper of the Flame. She is the woman who, in the darkest hours, lights a match and finds her way out of the dark tunnel. She is a source of inspiration, a lightworker, not only drawing on her own spark but reigniting the flames of others. Shadow work is integral to any form of healing, going into the dark recesses of our minds, the unconscious, the root of our troubles. When we are done with the darkness, it's the Hearth Keeper that pulls us out. She holds the flame while we make our ascent. Don't confuse shadow work with the complete dimming of your inner spark. You always have this inside of you; what matters is that you are conscious of it. Shadow work is about bringing the unconscious to the conscious, the darkness to the light. And it's the Hearth Keeper that carries the torch and keeps the flame lit so we can find our way out of the shadows.

It's important to recognize when we are living from a soul-aligned place because then, we can take action to do the things that give us purpose and meaning, thereby radiating our light for all to see. We end up attracting more prosperity when we allow our inner flames to shine brightly. This is the knowledge of the Hearth Keeper. You must do the things that light your soul on fire. You must feed the flames within. You must consciously decide not to let your lights go dim. Follow your heart. Find your passion. Tend to the hearth within your home, within you, and within the ones you love.

EMBODYING THE HEARTH KEEPER

Because the Hearth Keeper tends to the flames of her soul and home, her light burns brightly for all to see. She is a magnet, drawing in love and abundance. She is warm and welcoming. She makes others feel comfortable in her presence. She is not afraid to shine. She is unafraid of others seeing her light. To embody the Hearth Keeper and tend to your inner flame, you must allow yourself to be seen. So often, we are taught to conform and blend in. Sometimes we step aside to allow others to shine. We stay small and quiet, not wanting others to see us. But to heal, to truly live in your truth and become the Hearth Keeper, you must shine your light. It requires you to understand that there is enough space for everyone to shine. It's not a competition; no one should have control over how brightly you burn except for you. You control the radiance of your inner flame. You alone have power, purpose, and passion. Don't let others' words or actions deter you from constantly showing your spark.

SHADOW ASPECTS OF THE HEARTH KEEPER

The shadow aspect of the Hearth Keeper comes through in those who border along the lines of a people pleaser. These women are often so caught up in helping others and taking care of things that they neglect to take care of themselves. You can't shine your brightest and truly help others if you don't tend to your flames first. Just as you wouldn't put on someone else's oxygen mask before your own, you also can't allow others to dim your spark. Don't hide your inner flame from others because you are scared of being seen or feel the need to stay small. Remember to tend to your flame. Your glow alone will light the way for others.

This shadow aspect is also the lightworker spreading love and "positive vibes only" and refusing to do their shadow work. There must be a balance. Refusing to do the healing necessary on a spiritual journey is spiritual bypassing.

HEARTH KEEPER
REFLECTION QUESTIONS

0 What lights you up inside? What are you
passionate about?

0 What causes or charities do you support?

0 What gives your life meaning?

0 Do you allow yourself to burn bright and be seen? Or
do you let others take the lead?

0 How can you tend to your flames and become the
Hearth Keeper of your soul?

0 Look at your surroundings. Are they warm and inviting? Do they bring you comfort?

GODDESSES TO WORK WITH
THAT EMBODY THE HEARTH KEEPER

○ Hestia:

Greek goddess of hearth and home, Keeper of the Eternal Flame

○ Vesta:

Roman goddess of hearth and home, Keeper of the Eternal Flame

○ Hekate:

Greek goddess of the crossroads, magick, the night, and the moon; Queen of Witches; Torchbearer

○ Pele:

Hawaiian goddess of volcanos

○ Amaterasu:

Japanese goddess of the sun

○ Gabija:

Lithuanian fire goddess of hearth, home, and family

○ Hathor:

Egyptian goddess of women, the sky, fertility, and love

○ Yhi:

Australian Aboriginal goddess of light and creation

○ Sol:

Norse goddess of the sun

HEARTH KEEPER
RITUAL

Materials Needed:

 ⟡ Candle

The Hearth Keeper's main element is fire, so for this ritual, you'll need a candle. Light the candle and sit with it for as long as you need to, staring into its flame. Fire scrying is an ancient divination technique in which people glance into a fire to see images that pop up within the flames. Allow your gaze to soften and your body to relax. Do your best to enter a meditative state.

After focusing on the image of the flame in front of you, close your eyes. In this ritual, you want to connect to your inner flame, which is located in your solar plexus, right above your belly button. Breathe deep into this space. Imagine a flame within you. It might be dim at first, or it might burn bright like the flame before you. On each inhale, image your inner flame becoming bigger, hotter, and brighter. Allow it to stretch throughout your entire being, setting you on fire. Fire is an element of creation and destruction. Whatever has been holding you back, whatever doubts you carry, whatever you've been holding on to and are ready to release, allow this fire to burn it away. Allow your inner flame to cleanse your body. Your inner flame is not here to destroy you; its purpose in this ritual is to help burn away all those things that no longer serve you. Allow yourself to burn bright, melting away any impurities, self-doubt, or anything at all that's been bothering you. By cleansing yourself with this meditative fire, you are creating a blank slate and giving yourself permission to start again. Allow it to consume you. Allow it to reveal a way forward within its flames.

When you are done, picture the flames receding back into your solar plexus. Do not dim your light completely. Pull back the flames so they become one single flame, like that of the candle in front of you. The flames that raged around you are once again contained inside. Your inner flame is something that can never be put out. Anytime you want to connect with it, you may repeat this ritual. Anytime you feel like you are playing it small, holding on to too much, or have lost your zest and passion for life, reconnect with your inner flame. Play with making it bigger or smaller. Remember, you are in total control. Your inner flame is your personal spark. It can't destroy you; it can only help you by destroying things that aren't meant to be a part of you. It returns you to your true essence. Remember to nurture this flame within and feel it burn bright as you do things you love. Allow yourself to be seen.

THE DARK GODDESS

One of the most misunderstood archetypes is the Dark Goddess. People often confuse the term "dark" to mean "evil" or "bad." However, in this context, the darkness of the Dark Goddess means going into the shadows, the hidden, the unconscious. The Dark Goddess is one of raw, primal power. She is the liberator, the creator, the destroyer. She understands the cycles of death and rebirth. She herself has been reborn many times over, cutting ties with people and unshackling the bonds that were placed upon her by others or even by herself. She has shed her skin more than once. Like the phoenix, she is reborn from the ashes, becoming stronger and wiser with each resurrection. She harnesses her powerful emotions and uses them to create awe-inspiring beauty in her life. She goes fearlessly into the dark unknown, knowing she will find her answers.

The Dark Goddess is not an archetype that takes us to the dark side of life. She wants to liberate us from the falsehoods and lies we've grown up believing. She is an archetype of fierce love and radical truth. She is one of the most transformational archetypes to work with, especially during times when you feel stuck, for she is the archetype to call on that will burn everything to the ground for you to see the truth. She will destroy everything in your path so you can create your future. The Dark Goddess holds you in the highest capacity, accepting every inch of your being. She is the archetype that looks out at the world and sees clearly how backward we've built our lives, prioritizing greed over love, competition over kindness, perfectionism over acceptance, lies over truth.

She is the archetype to turn to when you need to work through all of your emotions. She represents the shadowy aspects of ourselves that come through. Sometimes these shadows are perceived as socially unacceptable, stemming from the way we were taught to act and speak at a very young age. The Dark Goddess can manifest through anger, frustration, or raw primal energy. She is a combination of all of those emotions that are deemed socially unacceptable yet are perfectly human, the shadowy aspects of ourselves we tend to suppress for fear of being judged. These may be characteristics, hobbies, feelings, or desires we might not feel comfortable sharing with others. Sometimes these things might come off as taboo. A lot of times, though, our shadow self is a mystery, even to us, because we have become so used to pushing it away. We hide it behind a door, lock it, and throw away the key, never wanting to accept it.

The Dark Goddess wants to liberate all of that. She holds a mirror up to you to uncover the truth. She wants to unbury those emotions, desires, and traits that make you who you are. The Dark Goddess calls us to express ourselves openly and freely. She is not afraid to speak up, because she knows what she says radiates with her divine truth. She embraces all aspects of her being, the dark and the light. The Dark Goddess is not afraid of being perceived as "wild," "crazy," "too much," "emotional," or "a bitch." She expresses herself fully because she knows if she doesn't, she isn't being true to herself.

The Dark Goddess is a feminine archetype that resides within us all. And although she is an archetype found across many cultures and mythologies, she is often misunderstood. She wants restitution for all the damage done to her and to the feminine within the collective. She is the archetype that is all-encompassing. She wants to speak freely, feel all of her emotions, and dance wildly when she wants. She is the archetype that has put fear in men because she has it all. She demands it all.

As the liberator, she wants to free you from the shackles placed on you by society, the shackles that tell you to fit into a box or follow the linear path everyone is "supposed to" take, like school, then marriage, then children. She wants to free you from the expectations to act a certain way and not be "too emotional," "too wild," or even "too much" for people to handle. She urges you to be too much, too emotional. She wants you to both ride on cloud nine and dive into the depths of your soul. She wants you to feel and scream and kick and punch (in a healthy way, of course) because that means you're actually living. She wants you to experience the fullness of life. You aren't meant to be complacent. You aren't meant to fit into a box. You are meant to expand like the rising tides of the ocean. You are meant to soar like an eagle. The Dark Goddess wants to liberate you from your ego and detach you from the feelings of fear, greed, and competition.

As a creator, the Dark Goddess wants you to recognize the power you have in creating the life you want. You are not a victim of your situation. You are capable of making the choices to change any circumstance you want. Why would you settle for the life you've been given if you aren't happy? What can you change to create the life you want?

The Dark Goddess asks us to get uncomfortable. She knows change never happens in our comfort zone. I believe the main reason many people fear the Dark Goddess is because she asks us to do the hard work, get uncomfortable, and face the things we've been avoiding. Once we do decide to confront those demons, she is there, loving us and carrying the torch as she guides us out of the shadows and back into the light. She holds our hand and gives us the strength to face those demons in the first place.

The Dark Goddess is the messenger from beyond, the goddess of death and rebirth. She values freedom and truth. She requires authenticity. She is the queen of the shadows, keeper of the mysteries. She understands that the only way to heal and step into your fierce feminine power is to walk the path through the shadows.

As a destroyer, the Dark Goddess honors the cycles of death and rebirth. To grow and change, you must shed your old skin. You must give up something to gain something. You must release the old version of yourself to become a newer version. This is the cyclical order of things. Something must be destroyed for something else to be created. It's how energy stays balanced. If you notice a lot of your friends are suddenly moving on without you or perhaps you choose not to be around them anymore, it's a sign you are making space for new people to come into your life. Honor the process. Just like life, death will always have a place in our world. It's never something to fear; it's just a signal for change.

EMBODYING THE DARK GODDESS

To embody the Dark Goddess and fully dive into this archetype, you must access your body wisdom. You must allow yourself to feel and go there. Feel all of your emotions as they arise, sit with them, and work through them. Get honest with yourself and dive deeper into the truth and mysteries of the Divine. The Dark Goddess is fearless; she is unafraid to go into the depths, the darkest parts of her being, to clear out the baggage that remains there. She will rage at the injustices done, she will seek to tear down the faulty structures to begin anew, and she will fiercely love everything in the process. She allows us to see the truth. She is ready for death, staring straight into its deep, piercing eyes, knowing that rebirth will greet her on the other side.

SHADOW ASPECTS OF THE DARK GODDESS

The shadow aspect of the Dark Goddess comes through when we find ourselves stuck in a phase of anger and rage. It's natural to go through many emotions when realizing that the societal or cultural restrictions that have been placed on us actually hinder us from being authentic. When we get stuck in this phase, though, rage turns into vengeance, and seeking retribution for the wrong done to us can cause us to become the "demon" society casts the Dark Goddess as. It's OK to sit with these emotions and take your time to move past them. But the Dark Goddess has your highest potential in mind; she holds nothing but love for you. If you are stuck in vengeance mode, ask yourself what you still need to work through. Head back into the shadows and get brutally honest with yourself.

DARK GODDESS
REFLECTION QUESTIONS

○ Have you ever been told you were "too much" or "too emotional"? How did that make you feel?

○ What parts of yourself do you tend to hide away from others?

○ Do you have any suppressed anger you haven't worked through?

○ Are there any societal expectations you wish to be liberated from?

○ Are there any past traumas or wounds you've been avoiding working through?

○ Do you allow yourself to feel all of your emotions freely?

GODDESSES TO WORK WITH
THAT EMBODY THE DARK GODDESS

- *O* Hekate:
  Greek goddess of the crossroads, magick, the night, and the moon; Queen of Witches

- *O* Morrigan:
  Celtic goddess of death, battle, and prophecy

- *O* Kali:
  Hindu goddess of time, death, and destruction

- *O* Persephone:
  Greek goddess of spring, Queen of the Underworld

- *O* Lilith:
  Dark moon goddess, Adam's first wife in Jewish folklore

- *O* Cerridwen:
  Celtic goddess of inspiration and rebirth, keeper of the cauldron

- *O* Medusa:
  Greek gorgon of power and sexuality

DARK GODDESS
RITUAL

This is a two-part ritual, so be sure to carve out enough uninterrupted time in your day to complete both parts together.

Materials Needed:

○ Mirror

○ The Dark Goddess playlist[2]

For the first part of this ritual, sit in front of a mirror and take in your reflection. Sans makeup, look into your eyes. Really look at yourself, your real, raw, authentic self. Notice the thoughts that arise. What comes up? How do you speak to yourself? Now is the time to face your truth. What in your life are you currently working toward? What have you been avoiding? Why? Devote as much time as you need to this first exercise. Allow yourself to get uncomfortable (if that's what arises for you). Take this time to honestly talk to yourself and work through whatever you need to.

When you are ready, turn on the Dark Goddess playlist I created specifically for this exercise. Start to sink into the music.

2 The Dark Goddess playlist can be found at www.courtneytiffany.com/femininearchetypes

Allow the beats of the drums to vibrate through you. Allow yourself to dance and move freely. Express yourself in whatever way you wish. Use this time to move through any emotions that came up for you during the mirror exercise. If it was love and admiration, then dance and embrace the beauty of your body. If it was anger, doubts, or fears, then move your body in a way that helps you purge those emotions. Open up to Shakti energy here. Allow the flow of the serpent to move through you. Dance to scare off your demons. Dance to embrace your true nature. Dance like the world is on fire and you are the only one who can save it.

Moving your physical body allows you to move your internal energy. Scream, cry, laugh, shout, emote it all! Dance with the Dark Goddess. Dance with *your* Dark Goddess. Let her liberate you. Invite her love, truth, acceptance, fierceness, and fearlessness into you. This is your metamorphosis. Call on her to guide you through the shadows. Ask her to help you get rid of all the baggage you've been holding on to. Surrender to her dance, then surrender some more.

Stay here in this energy for as long as you'd like. Feel her power radiate through you. Feel her strength as you move through the darkness. Do not be afraid. Pay attention to how the energy of the Dark Goddess varies from the other archetypes you've explored. When you are ready to close out the ritual, thank the Dark Goddess for appearing to you in whatever form she did. You may wish to journal or write down a few thoughts that arose during the ritual. These are always beneficial to help you as you continue along in your shadow work. And one day, you'll be able to look back on these notes and see how far you've come. Remember, shadow work is never easy, but it's the most rewarding thing you will ever do for yourself.

THE MYSTIC

There are two types of whales in the world: toothed whales, such as the orca and sperm whale, and baleen whales, like the humpback or gray whale. The scientific name for baleen whales is Mysticeti, which I've always found interesting. It reminds me of the word "mystic." Whales are the largest animals on our planet, and they have the longest migration of any animal, yet they are gentle giants, gracefully swimming along, singing their serene songs, and diving into the depths of the ocean. The entire experience seems mystical, far away from where I am currently writing this book, somewhere in the Sonoran Desert. Still, the Mystic in me dreams of being that humpback whale, dancing along the ocean currents, not concerned with time or space.

It's the Mystic archetype that allows us to travel without ever leaving our homes. The Mystic is the wisdom seeker and the obtainer of knowledge, wanting to understand the ways of the world. She values truth above everything else. She's on an endless quest for knowledge, yearning to understand everything in a deeper, more profound way. She doesn't want surface-level chitchat; she craves to see into the depths of your soul. She prefers to witness the inner workings of one's mind and heart. She asks the hard questions, not who or when but how and why. Why is this being revealed? How can I dig deeper? What is the reason behind it all?

The Mystic in us understands that there is more to this life than basic human living, the day-to-day stuff we often occupy our time and energy with. She trusts her intuition completely. Her goal is to obtain spiritual liberation, stand in pure divine presence, and become one with the pulse of the Universe. She values solitude. The Mystic's life is in service to the Divine; she is more interested in letting go of all ego attachments than obtaining power. She is in pursuit of inner peace. She builds her life on mindfulness and self-awareness. She seeks union with the anima mundi. She is perfectly fine putting aside rational thoughts for an unexplainable experience.

The Mystic archetype seeks to understand the ways of the world. She has the ability to surrender completely to the Divine, for she understands the laws of the Universe. She has come to accept that she is not in control but merely along for the ride. She easily adapts to any situation because she knows everything that gets thrown her way serves a purpose. Her life is built on faith and trust in the Divine. She is more concerned with inner fulfillment than external goals.

The Mystic differs from the Priestess in that she is not a guide. The Mystic is not concerned with teaching others but rather with being a channel for divine guidance. She may turn her insights and visions into art, music, or poetry and share divine messages via those outlets. She may inspire others with her devotion, but she is not in a position of leadership. The Mystic may spread divine love through selfless acts of service. She may give to others as a way of passing along divine messages or guidance. She is a conduit of divine energy, an oracle or seer.

The Mystic may often find herself battling her inner turmoil. She yearns to travel to different realms and astral planes, explore a higher consciousness, and seek divine alignment, but she is only human. She may struggle to keep her feet firmly on the ground. The Mystic wants to shed falsehoods and limited thinking and obtain enlightenment, but the reality is we are trapped in our physical bodies. We are human, we have emotions, and we don't live in a world where we can be in complete soul alignment all the time. She must accept the limitations of her physical form.

EMBODYING THE MYSTIC

When you embody the Mystic, you must allow yourself to surrender to the divine flow of things. You must detach from your ego and allow yourself to completely trust in divine timing. You might see messages from the Universe in various signs or symbols, whether through animal guides, angel numbers, or other synchronicities. The Mystic is in tune with her higher self and spirit guides. She understands that the Universe/God is always trying to communicate with us, and that it's up to us to pay attention. You must possess a level of self-awareness that allows you to heal rather than give in to suffering. There is a level of detachment and emotional independence with the Mystic to see things through a higher perspective. She has brought this level of consciousness into every aspect of her life, including her career, her relationships, and what she chooses to consume.

To tap into the Mystic, you needn't be so concerned about fulfilling a destiny or your life's purpose as much as enjoying your day-to-day life. The Mystic understands that she is allowed to fully express herself and shouldn't be concerned about the little daily stresses. She is highly intuitive and trusts she will be guided to where she needs to go. She has learned to ride the waves and sing her song, much like the Mysticeti.

SHADOW ASPECTS OF THE MYSTIC

When the Mystic is in the shadow, she is lost in other realms, forgetting to keep herself grounded. Her deep introversion can make her somewhat removed from life. Her head is in the clouds, and she uses her divine channeling gifts as a form of escapism. She might even become judgmental of others who are not on the same path as her or as devoted as her. To come out of the shadows, she must reconnect with her humanness. Life is a dance between the Divine and human living. As with everything, there must be a balance.

MYSTIC
REFLECTION QUESTIONS

———————

O Can you learn to ride the waves of life?

O Are you able to surrender more to the ways of the Universe and release control?

O What attachments do you have to your physical world?

O Are you comfortable with opening up your channel to receive divine messages?

O Do you trust your intuition? How can you develop it further?

GODDESSES TO WORK WITH
THAT EMBODY THE MYSTIC

O Hestia:

Greek goddess of hearth and home, Keeper of the
Eternal Flame

O Vesta:

Roman goddess of hearth and home, Keeper of the
Eternal Flame

O Sarasvati:

Hindu goddess of knowledge, the arts, and music

O Sophia:

Gnostic mother goddess of wisdom

MYSTIC
RITUAL

To really connect with the Mystic, you must be able to open up a channel of communication with the Divine. Each and every one of us possesses the ability to communicate with things that seem beyond this realm. Right now, your belief in spirit guides, God/Divine, etc. is irrelevant, but I have a feeling that if you've picked up this book, you have some notion of different realms. Sit in a comfortable seated position, preferably on a pillow or an extra cushion, with your legs crossed and touching the ground. You want to be able to straighten your spine and sit as tall as you comfortably can for this ritual.

When you are ready, start by sinking into your body and the present moment. Take a few deep, cleansing breaths, feeling your chest rise and fall with each inhale and exhale. Begin to clear your mind. When you are ready, imagine a beam of bright, white light pulsating down from the heavens into your crown. Imagine your crown, or the top of your head, opening up to receive this light. This is pure Divine/God/Source/universal light. Pull it down and into your body. Imagine this white light streaming inside your entire being. On the inhale, feel as it expands into your body, across your chest, all the way to the tips of your fingers, and down to your toes. Breathe in this pure divine energy and allow it to fill you up and transmute any doubts or fears you may be carrying. Allow it to burn away the stresses of your daily life.

If you feel called to ask for guidance, ask a specific question or request assistance. Now is the time to ask for anything you may need. Once you do, simply wait. Be still. Stay present. You may get your answer via an intuitive knowing, a feeling in your body, or you may hear it. If nothing comes to you, that's OK. Now may not be the time for an answer, but ask the Divine to send you a sign and keep your eyes open in the days following for your answer.

Sit here as long as you need to. When you are ready to close the channel, simply feel as the light gathers into a straight, bright, white beam and travels up and out of your crown. Close the energetic door you opened on the top of your head, and open your eyes.

THE CRONE

The archetype of immense wisdom is one that deserves much more respect than we give her credit for. The Crone is the wise woman, the completion of the triple goddess. She has planned and gathered her materials, brought new life and creations into this world, mothered and nurtured them, and has now released them to be on their own. No longer the eager Maiden ready to start her journey, and having already completed her motherhood, she is now on her own, enjoying her solitude. Within the moon's phases, the Crone is associated with the waning moon. She represents a time of retreat, a cycle slowly coming to an end. But do not discredit her, for she has seen many things and is the wisest of us all. She has seen her creations take life without her, separate from her now. Some believe you can't enter Cronehood until after menopause, a natural stage in the lives of women. Yet I believe, as I've said before, the archetypes are available to us all at any time and any age. She shouldn't just be depicted as the old wise woman with gray hair. She is available to anyone who has learned a lesson and mentors others.

The Crone gains her wisdom through experience. She uses wisdom and judgment, combining her head and her heart to make decisions. She has witnessed a lot in her life and applies what she has learned to current situations. She recognizes that there are always opportunities to learn. The wise woman has lived through many years of trials and tribulations and has come out on the other side wiser and stronger. She has many stories to tell. The wisdom of the wise woman is not something that can be taught; it can only be gained through experience, so don't block yourself from experiencing the Crone by failing to see the lessons waiting to be learned.

To embody the Crone, you must enter a meditative state of mind, a place of reflection. She provides for you an opportunity to look back at all that you have accomplished thus far—all the mistakes you made along the way, all the times you needed to course correct, the moments when you stood up for yourself and others, the times you were courageous, and the times when you faced hard decisions. All of these moments have added up to the wisdom you now carry within you. The Crone possesses a certain mindset of autonomy, of living only for herself. She does not do things to please others. She only lives to please herself. She has learned that the opinions of others are of no concern to her. She understands she can only control her actions, thoughts, and words, and she is not responsible for those of others. She does what makes her happy. Long gone are the days of people pleasing and seeking validation outside of herself. The Crone has learned that putting her energy into someone else can be stressful and draining, so she chooses to live on her own terms.

The Crone has so much to teach us. She sees the value in the cycle of life and death. She herself has experienced many endings in her life. She knows the beauty of release, of letting go of things, in order to make space for the new. She understands that nothing is permanent in this life, things are always coming and going. She is patient with this rhythm. She is familiar with the in between, the liminal spaces and the voids within the cycles. The Crone welcomes death, knowing the next chapter awaits.

I urge you to not only connect with your inner Crone but also with other women in your life who are your mentors and may embody the Crone. Seek out the wise women in your circle and call on them for advice. My childhood was spent in a geriatric-based community; I was surrounded by my extended family, mainly all the siblings of my grandparents (there were a lot of them). I had many great aunts and uncles, and I spent so much time with all of them growing up that I learned to listen to their stories. Those days were some of the best of my life, and I wish I had known when I was younger to take more time and ask more questions, to understand more of the ways of the world. Many of them had seen war, depression, abundance, and everything in between. Because I grew up this way, I oftentimes feel more comfortable with Crones than with peers my own age. A lot of them called me an old soul when I was a child, but I think I recognized the wisdom within them. It breaks my heart that we live in a society that separates people as they get older. When you reach a certain age, you are given a new label and have separate communities to live in. Why aren't we including them? Why don't we give back to them toward the end of their lives the same way they sacrificed for us at the beginning of ours?

The Crone has been cast out of society in a lot of ways due to the way we fail to honor senior citizens. In the media, she can be portrayed as the hag, the old crazy woman, or the loner. We don't value her the way we should. We should be doing more to accept the wise woman. The Crone has seen more than anyone else in our lives, so why isn't she treated with more respect? We should be putting the Crone on a pedestal. She is the keeper of wisdom and magic. She understands how to best access the mysteries of the Divine. She has a responsibility to accumulate wisdom and share it with others so that it might not be lost. Yet, we are treating her in the exact opposite way. We put her in a home and only visit when it's convenient for us. What is it about the Crone that makes society write her off? There is so much value in multi-generational living. Not only does it teach our children to respect and honor our elders, but they have the chance to witness what it means to fully live life. They see the differences and pros of various ages.

Honor the Crone by listening. Listen to other women, accumulate wisdom and experiences, and turn around to be a mentor for someone else. Recognize that we can all provide value to the collective experience. Share your stories, traditions, and wisdom with the next generation.

EMBODYING THE CRONE

Embody the Crone by honoring your wisdom. Take a look back on your life and notice all that you have learned and achieved. Take pride in the wisdom and experiences you've accumulated. Honor your story. Honor the cycle of life, death, and rebirth. How many times have you been reborn? How many chances have you been given to start again? How many chapters have you closed? Sit in contemplation and reflection. Lean into the gifts of the Crone, the wisdom, the memories. Be OK with knowing the answers and solutions without knowing *how* you know them. Some things can't be explained by logic or reason. The Crone has learned to trust her intuitive knowing, and she allows it to guide her and her direction in life.

SHADOW ASPECTS OF THE CRONE

The Crone in her shadow phase comes through when we are unwilling to learn anything new. Just because someone has lived through experiences and is knowledgeable in many areas doesn't mean there isn't anything left for them to know. We are all students of life, and there is always more to learn. The Crone who is done learning creates a ripple of sadness for all who seek her wisdom. Other shadow aspects include bitterness, being critical of others, or tearing people down. She may be stuck in a loop of regrets rather than appreciating the life she has already lived.

CRONE
REFLECTION QUESTIONS

O What women in your life do you turn to for advice?

O Looking back at your life and experiences so far, what are some lessons you've learned along the way?

O What advice would you give to your younger self?

O Are there things in life you simply know without knowing how you know them?

O Do you harbor any fears about the death and rebirth cycle? If so, why?

GODDESSES TO WORK WITH
THAT EMBODY THE CRONE

○ Hekate:

Greek goddess of the crossroads, magick, the night, and the moon; Queen of Witches

○ Macha:

Celtic goddess of horses, battle, and fertility; part of the Morrigan triple goddess

○ Baba Yaga:

Slavic goddess of death and regeneration

○ Cerridwen:

Celtic goddess of inspiration and rebirth, keeper of the cauldron

CRONE
RITUAL

The wisdom of the Crone can be shared through listening and storytelling. Spend some time with your elders. Ask them to tell you about the times of their youth, times of hardship and suffering, and times of celebration. Listen. Really listen. Take in their body language as they open up with their stories. What are the lessons they had to learn in their lifetimes? What are the stories that made the biggest impact on them? What stories are they choosing to share?

If you don't have an elder to talk to, write down your story. Share a time you experienced pain, a dark night of the soul. How did you overcome it? What are the significant moments of your life thus far?

The Crone shares her wisdom through story. If you feel called to, you may share your stories with your children or a friend. To experience the true magic of the Crone, light a fire and gather people around for a night of storytelling. Don't read from a book; share from your heart. Ask each person to share a story with the group. Make it a night of remembrance, connection, and vulnerability. Honor your own wisdom and the lessons you've learned thus far. Nothing is too small or insignificant.

CONCLUSION

It's my hope that by reading this book, you've learned something new about the archetypes you possess. I hope it has opened a door for you to explore these parts of yourself further. Perhaps not all of the archetypes stood out at once, but I'm glad that the few that did have piqued your curiosity. I encourage you to explore these archetypes even further. What we discussed in this book has barely scratched the surface of what the archetypes possess. Tug on those threads that call to you, then pull on them even more. Notice how each one feels in your body.

We are cyclical creatures, riding the waves of life, and at different points in our lives, we are required to call forth different parts of our being. All of the archetypes presented offer a way for us not only to get to know ourselves on a deeper level but also to connect with the pulsating, creative energy of the Divine Feminine. Continue to explore the various ways the archetypes are expressed within you. See how they want to manifest through you, and receive the gifts and mysteries they possess. The ways of the Divine Feminine can best be learned through embodiment. Tune into the energetic frequency of each archetype, get to know them over time, and watch as you grow more confident and intuitive in your way of living.

Women are beautiful, complex creatures who are comprised of so many gifts. Each archetype has presented lessons for me and has taught me things about myself I had forgotten or had not yet explored. It's my hope that the lessons I've shared have sparked something in you as well. Hopefully, they have opened your mind to a new way of living and being and you will continue exploring these new parts of yourself, as well as the goddesses attributed to each one.

Learning about the feminine archetypes in my spiritual practice is what led me to experience my first kundalini awakening. They awakened the snake coiled deep within me, and I feel like I've been dancing ever since. If you didn't connect with all of the archetypes, that's OK. Just connecting with one of them is enough to unlock parts of yourself and learn more about who you are as a person and what you are capable of. Each archetype gifts us with her unique perspective, so continue to tap into that thread of your being and watch as your connection to the mysteries deepens even further.

Remember, all of these archetypes live within you. In this book, we've explored thirteen of them, but there are hundreds more out there. Continue to dive deep and discover more about yourself, for the true path of spirituality is to know thyself. Explore, play, and embody. And most importantly, let the Divine lead the way.

ACKNOWLEDGEMENTS

I am beyond blessed to have found a wonderful and inspiring team of women to help me bring my vison to life. My amazing and brilliant editor Lyric Dodson, thank you for being patient with me as I worked through the many drafts of this book. Your encouragement to go back to the drawing board and response to each and every note made this a book I will forever be proud of.

To my formatter Ines, your attention to detail never ceases to amaze me, and many thanks to spearheading the final production of this book.

Thank you to my cover designer Margo for bringing my vision to life.

Thanks to Mary Lanham for proofreading, your thoughtful notes were so appreciated.

I'm in deep gratitude to all the women in my life who are constantly cheering me on, sharing my work, and supporting me in the background.

And special thanks to my husband Ryan, for sharing this life with me, for your endless support, for never judging my "obscure" interests, and listening to all of my rantings about the archetypes.

To my little wildflower and daughter Daphne, for whom this book is dedicated to, I hope you never shy away from your magnetic radiance. You are the kindest, most gentle soul, and I hope one day you too will learn to stand in your brilliance and truth. You are a powerful light my darling. Keep shining on.

ABOUT THE AUTHOR

Courtney Tiffany is a writer, intuitive, and modern Priestess of the Divine Feminine. She is the Founder of the Monthly Goddess Alignment. Author of Journey to Soul, and creator of the Goddess Affirmations Oracle Deck. She is dedicated to helping others gain clarity, access Shakti, and reconnect with their true essence and soul wisdom. She teaches women internationally how to connect to the Divine Feminine via goddess spirituality and archetypal embodiment. She lives in Arizona with her husband, two children, and menagerie of pets.

To get the latest information and learn more about Courtney's current projects, subscribe to her newsletter at: www.courtneytiffany.com

If you've enjoyed this book please consider leaving a review on Amazon or Goodreads.

RESOURCES TO DEEPEN YOUR JOURNEY

ARCHETYPAL ACTIVATIONS

If you are wanting to go deeper into archetypal embodiment and to explore this work further, you can join Courtney inside the Monthly Goddess Alignment. Inside you'll find activations for each of the thirteen feminine archetypes, in which she takes you through a guided journey to connect with each thread of Shakti—not only helping you to embody the archetype within yourself, but also offering support and community.

You can join the Monthly Goddess Alignment sisterhood at www.patreon.com/authorcourtneytiffany.

PLAYLISTS

Music is a great tool to help you drop into your body wisdom and allow the flow of the Divine Feminine to rise up. You can find playlists curated for each of the thirteen archetypes available for free at www.courtneytiffany.com/femininearchetypes.

MORE INFORMATION

You can also find more information regarding the Divine Feminine and various goddesses and archetypes on Courtney's website and social media pages:

Website: www.courtneytiffany.com

Instagram: @authorcourtneytiffany

Facebook: @authorcourtneytiffany

Patreon: @authorcourtneytiffany

Youtube: Courtney Tiffany

Printed in Great Britain
by Amazon

84841003R00113